ETHIOPIA

ETHIOPIA IN THE MODERN WORLD

JOHN G. HALL

INTRODUCTORY ESSAY BY
Dr. Richard E. Leakey
Chairman, Wildlife Clubs
of Kenya Association
✢

AFTERWORD BY
Deirdre Shields

CHELSEA HOUSE PUBLISHERS
Philadelphia
In association with Covos Day Books, South Africa

CHELSEA HOUSE PUBLISHERS

EDITOR IN CHIEF Sally Cheney
DIRECTOR OF PRODUCTION Kim Shinners
CREATIVE MANAGER Takeshi Takahashi
MANUFACTURING MANAGER Diann Grasse

Staff for ETHIOPIA

EDITOR Lee M. Marcott
PRODUCTION ASSISTANT Jaimie Winkler
COVER DESIGN Emiliano Begnardi
SERIES DESIGNER Keith Trego

The Chelsea House World Wide Web address is http://www.chelseahouse.com
First Printing
1 3 5 7 9 8 6 4 2

Library of Congress Cataloging-in-Publication Data

Hall, John G., 1950-
    Ethiopia / John G. Hall.
        p. cm. -- (Exploration of Africa, the emerging nations)
     Summary: Photographs and text look at the past, development, and present
culture of Ethiopia and its inhabitants.
        Includes bibliographical references (p.) and index.
     ISBN 0-7910-5745-3
        1. Ethiopia—History—Juvenile literature. [1. Ethiopia.] I. Title.
    II. Series.
    DT381 .H34 2002
    963—dc21
                                                               2002004895

The photographs in this book are from the Royal Geographical Society Picture Library. Most are being published for the first time.

The Royal Geographical Society Picture Library provides an unrivaled source of over half a million images of
peoples and landscapes from around the globe. Photographs date from the 1840s onwards on a variety of sub-
jects including the British Colonial Empire, deserts, exploration, indigenous peoples, landscapes, remote desti-
nations, and travel.

Photography, beginning with the daguerreotype in 1839, is only marginally younger than the Society, which
encouraged its explorers to use the new medium from its earliest days. From the remarkable mid-19th century
black-and-white photographs to color transparencies of the late 20th century, the focus of the collection is not the
generic stock shot but the portrayal of man's resilience, adaptability, and mobility in remote parts of the world.

In organizing this project, we have incurred many debts of gratitude. Our first, though, is to the professional staff
of the Picture Library for their generous assistance, especially to Joanna Scadden, Picture Library Manager.

CONTENTS

EXPLORATION OF AFRICA: THE EMERGING NATIONS

THE DARK CONTINENT

DR. RICHARD E. LEAKEY

THE CONCEPT OF AFRICAN exploration has been greatly influenced by the hero status given to the European adventurers and missionaries who went off to Africa in the last century. Their travels and travails were certainly extraordinary and nobody can help but be impressed by the tremendous physical and intellectual courage that was so much a characteristic of people such as Livingstone, Stanley, Speke, and Baker, to name just a few. The challenges and rewards that Africa offered, both in terms of commerce and also "saved souls," inspired people to take incredible risks and endure personal suffering to a degree that was probably unique to the exploration of Africa.

I myself was fortunate enough to have had the opportunity to organize one or two minor expeditions to remote spots in Africa where there were no roads or airfields and marching with porters and/or camels was the best option at the time. I have also had the thrill of being with people untouched and often unmoved by contact with Western or other technologically based cultures, and these experiences remain for me amongst the most exciting and salutary of my life. With the contemporary revolution in technology, there will be few if any such opportunities again. Indeed I often find myself slightly saddened by the realization that were life ever discovered on another planet, exploration would doubtless be done by remote sensing and making full use of artificial, digital intelligence. At least it is unlikely to be in my lifetime and this is a relief!

ETHIOPIA

Notwithstanding all of this, I believe that the age of exploration and discovery in Africa is far from over. The future offers incredible opportunities for new discoveries that will push back the frontiers of knowledge. This endeavor will of course not involve exotic and arduous journeys into malaria-infested tropical swamps, but it will certainly require dedication, team work, public support, and a conviction that the rewards to be gained will more than justify the efforts and investment.

EARLY EXPLORERS

Many of us were raised and educated at school with the belief that Africa, the so-called Dark Continent, was actually discovered by early European travelers and explorers. The date of this "discovery" is difficult to establish, and anyway a distinction has always had to be drawn between northern Africa and the vast area south of the Sahara. The Romans certainly had information about the continent's interior as did others such as the Greeks. A diverse range of traders ventured down both the west coast and the east coast from at least the ninth century, and by the tenth century Islam had taken root in a number of new towns and settlements established by Persian and Arab interests along the eastern tropical shores. Trans-African trade was probably under way well before this time, perhaps partly stimulated by external interests.

Close to the beginning of the first millennium, early Christians were establishing the Coptic church in the ancient kingdom of Ethiopia and at other coastal settlements along Africa's northern Mediterranean coast. Along the west coast of Africa, European trade in gold, ivory, and people was well established by the sixteenth century. Several hundred years later, early in the 19th century, the systematic penetration and geographical exploration of Africa was undertaken by Europeans seeking geographical knowledge and territory and looking for opportunities not only for commerce but for the chance to spread the Gospel. The extraordinary narratives of some of the journeys of early European travelers and adventurers in Africa are a vivid reminder of just how recently Africa has become embroiled in the power struggles and vested interests of non-Africans.

THE DARK CONTINENT

AFRICA'S GIFT TO THE WORLD

My own preoccupation over the past thirty years has been to study human prehistory, and from this perspective it is very clear that Africa was never "discovered" in the sense in which so many people have been and, perhaps, still are being taught. Rather, it was Africans themselves who found that there was a world beyond their shores.

Prior to about two million years ago, the only humans or proto-humans in existence were confined to Africa; as yet, the remaining world had not been exposed to this strange mammalian species, which in time came to dominate the entire planet. It is no trivial matter to recognize the cultural implications that arise from this entirely different perspective of Africa and its relationship to the rest of humanity.

How many of the world's population grow up knowing that it was in fact African people who first moved and settled in southern Europe and Central Asia and migrated to the Far East? How many know that Africa's principal contribution to the world is in fact humanity itself? These concepts are quite different from the notion that Africa was only "discovered" in the past few hundred years and will surely change the commonly held idea that somehow Africa is a "laggard," late to come onto the world stage.

It could be argued that our early human forebears—the *Homo erectus* who moved out of Africa—have little or no bearing on the contemporary world and its problems. I disagree and believe that the often pejorative thoughts that are associated with the Dark Continent and dark skins, as well as with the general sense that Africans are somehow outside the mainstream of human achievement, would be entirely negated by the full acceptance of a universal African heritage for all of humanity. This, after all, is the truth that has now been firmly established by scientific inquiry.

The study of human origins and prehistory will surely continue to be important in a number of regions of Africa and this research must continue to rank high on the list of relevant ongoing exploration and discovery. There is still much to be learned about the early stages of human development, and the age of the "first humans"—the first bipedal apes—has not been firmly established. The current hypothesis is that prior to five million years ago there were no bipeds, and this would mean that humankind is only five million years old. Beyond Africa, there were no humans until just two million years ago, and this is a consideration that political leaders and people as a whole need to bear in mind.

RECENT HISTORY

When it comes to the relatively recent history of Africa's contemporary people, there is still considerable ignorance. The evidence suggests that there were major migrations of people within the continent during the past 5,000 years, and the impact of the introduction of domestic stock must have been quite considerable on the way of life of many of Africa's people. Early settlements and the beginnings of nation states are, as yet, poorly researched and recorded. Although archaeological studies have been undertaken in Africa for well over a hundred years, there remain more questions than answers.

One question of universal interest concerns the origin and inspiration for the civilization of early Egypt. The Nile has, of course, offered opportunities for contacts between the heart of Africa and the Mediterranean seacoast, but very little is known about human settlement and civilization in the upper reaches of the Blue and White Nile between 4,000 and 10,000 years ago. We do know that the present Sahara Desert is only about 10,000 years old; before this Central Africa was wetter and more fertile, and research findings have shown that it was only during the past 10,000 years that Lake Turkana in the northern Kenya was isolated from the Nile system. When connected, it would have been an excellent connection between the heartland of the continent and the Mediterranean.

Another question focuses on the extensive stone-walled villages and towns in Southern Africa. The Great Zimbabwe is but one of thousands of standing monuments in East, Central, and Southern Africa that attest to considerable human endeavor in Africa long before contact with Europe or Arabia. The Neolithic period and Iron Age still offer very great opportunities for exploration and discovery.

As an example of the importance of history, let us look at the modern South Africa where a visitor might still be struck by the not-too-subtle representation of a past that, until a few years ago, only "began" with the arrival of Dutch settlers some 400 years back. There are, of course, many pre-Dutch sites, including extensive fortified towns where kingdoms and nation states had thrived hundreds of years before contact with Europe; but this evidence has been poorly documented and even more poorly portrayed.

Few need to be reminded of the sparseness of Africa's precolonial written history. There are countless cultures and historical narratives that have been recorded only as oral history and legend. As postcolonial Africa further consolidates itself, history must be reviewed and deepened to incorporate the realities of precolonial human settlement as well as foreign contact. Africa's identity and self-respect is closely linked to this.

One of the great tragedies is that African history was of little interest to the early European travelers who were in a hurry and had no brief to document the details of the people they came across during their travels. In the basements of countless European museums, there are stacked shelves of African "curios"—objects taken from the people but seldom documented in terms of the objects' use, customs, and history.

There is surely an opportunity here for contemporary scholars to do something. While much of Africa's precolonial past has been obscured by the slave trade, colonialism, evangelism, and modernization, there remains an opportunity, at least in some parts of the continent, to record what still exists. This has to be one of the most vital frontiers for African exploration and discovery as we approach the end of this millennium. Some of the work will require trips to the field, but great gains could be achieved by a systematic and coordinated effort to record the inventories of European museums and archives. The Royal Geographical Society could well play a leading role in this chapter of African exploration. The compilation of a central data bank on what is known and what exists would, if based on a coordinated initiative to record the customs and social organization of Africa's remaining indigenous peoples, be a huge contribution to the heritage of humankind.

MEDICINES AND FOODS

On the African continent itself, there remain countless other areas for exploration and discovery. Such endeavors will be achieved without the fanfare of great expeditions and high adventure as was the case during the last century and they should, as far as possible, involve exploration and discovery of African frontiers by Africans themselves. These frontiers are not geographic: they are boundaries of knowledge in the sphere of Africa's home-grown cultures and natural world.

Indigenous knowledge is a very poorly documented subject in many parts of the world, and Africa is a prime example of a continent where centuries of accumulated local knowledge is rapidly disappearing in the face of modernization. I believe, for example, that there is much to be learned about the use of wild African plants for both medicinal and nutritional purposes. Such knowledge, kept to a large extent as the experience and memory of elders in various indigenous communities, could potentially have far-reaching benefits for Africa and for human-ity as a whole.

The importance of new remedies based on age-old medicines can-not be underestimated. Over the past two decades, international com-panies have begun to take note and to exploit certain African plants for pharmacological preparations. All too often, Africa has not been the beneficiary of these "discoveries," which are, in most instances, noth-ing more than the refinement and improvement of traditional African medicine. The opportunities for exploration and discovery in this area are immense and will have assured economic return on investment. One can only hope that such work will be in partnership with the peo-ple of Africa and not at the expense of the continent's best interests.

Within the same context, there is much to be learned about the tradi-tional knowledge of the thousands of plants that have been utilized by different African communities for food. The contemporary world has become almost entirely dependent, in terms of staple foods, on the cul-tivation of only six principal plants: corn, wheat, rice, yams, potatoes, and bananas. This cannot be a secure basis to guarantee the food requirements of more than five billion people.

Many traditional food plants in Africa are drought resistant and might well offer new alternatives for large-scale agricultural develop-ment in the years to come. Crucial to this development is finding out what African people used before exotics were introduced. In some rural areas of the continent, it is still possible to learn about much of this by talking to the older generation. It is certainly a great shame that some of the early European travelers in Africa were ill equipped to study and record details of diet and traditional plant use, but I am sure that, although it is late, it is not too late. The compilation of a pan-African database on what is known about the use of the continent's plant resources is a vital matter requiring action.

VANISHING SPECIES

In the same spirit, there is as yet a very incomplete inventory of the continent's other species. The inevitable trend of bringing land into productive management is resulting in the loss of unknown but undoubtedly large numbers of species. This genetic resource may be invaluable to the future of Africa and indeed humankind, and there really is a need for coordinated efforts to record and understand the continent's biodiversity.

In recent years important advances have been made in the study of tropical ecosystems in Central and South America, and I am sure that similar endeavors in Africa would be rewarding. At present, Africa's semi-arid and highland ecosystems are better understood than the more diverse and complex lowland forests, which are themselves under particular threat from loggers and farmers. The challenges of exploring the biodiversity of the upper canopy in the tropical forests, using the same techniques that are now used in Central American forests, are fantastic and might also lead to eco-tourist developments for these areas in the future.

It is indeed an irony that huge amounts of money are being spent by the advanced nations in an effort to discover life beyond our own planet, while at the same time nobody on this planet knows the extent and variety of life here at home. The tropics are especially relevant in this regard and one can only hope that Africa will become the focus of renewed efforts of research on biodiversity and tropical ecology.

AN AFROCENTRIC VIEW

Overall, the history of Africa has been presented from an entirely Eurocentric or even Caucasocentric perspective, and until recently this has not been adequately reviewed. The penetration of Africa, especially during the last century, was important in its own way; but today the realities of African history, art, culture, and politics are better known. The time has come to regard African history in terms of what has happened in Africa itself, rather than simply in terms of what non-African individuals did when they first traveled to the continent.

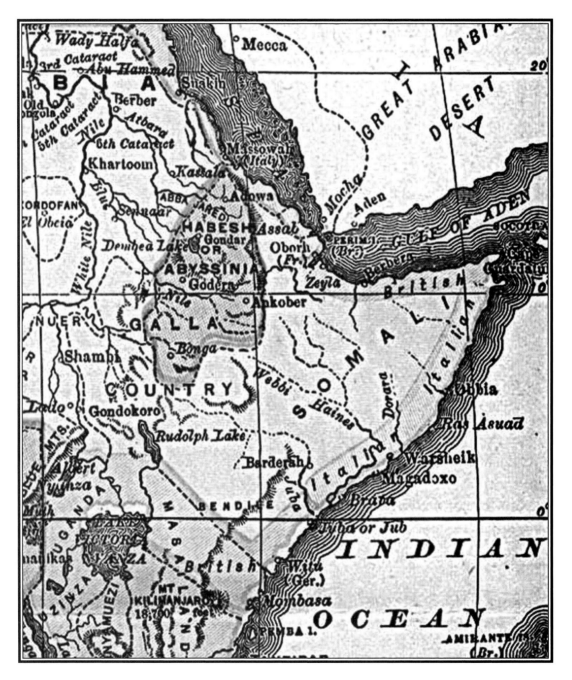

Map of Ethiopia, c. 1890

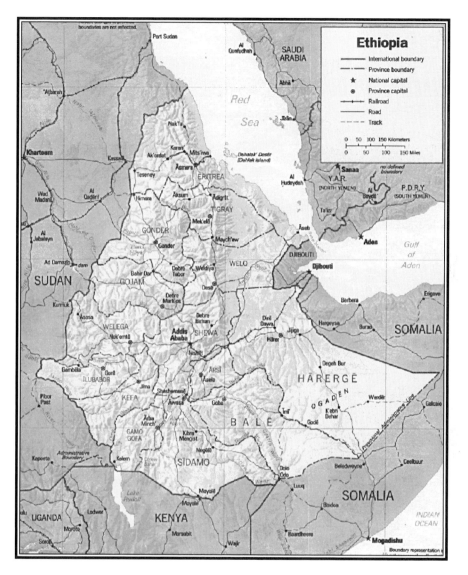

Modern map of Ethiopia

Ethiopian Woman and Child, c. 1895   *It is difficult to distinguish between Abyssinia and Ethiopia. In general, Abyssinia is the older name for Ethiopia. After more than a century of feudal anarchy, Yohannes IV became emperor of Ethiopia in 1872. This year is used to date the beginning of modern Ethiopia. This photograph was taken by L. Naretti, an Italian professional photographer who lived in Massawa, the main Eritrean port city on the Red Sea. Naretti's photographs were donated to the Royal Geographical Society in 1901 by G. P. Devey, who served as British vice-consul for Van, located in eastern Turkey, in the 1890s and later in Massawa. L. Naretti labeled this photograph "a country woman carrying child."*

THE GLORY OF KINGS

Ethiopia shall soon stretch out her hands unto God.
Psalms 68:31

What did Jamaican reggae singer Bob Marley, Black Nationalist leader Marcus Garvey, and Emperor Haile Selassie I of Ethiopia have in common? They all shared a deep reverence for the *Kebra Nagast*, the sacred text of Ethiopian Christians and Jamaican Rastafarians. For nearly a thousand years the people of Ethiopia have held this book in the highest esteem. It contains the prophecy that Ethiopia and its people are the chosen ones of God.

Kebra Nagast, or "The Glory of Kings," is a thirteenth-century manuscript that retells the legendary and historical events of the Ethiopian people. It contains the earliest surviving version of the story of the queen of Sheba and her relationship with King Solomon, their son Menelik, and the eventual abduction of the Ark of the Covenant from the First Temple in Jerusalem.

In its importance to the Ethiopian people, the *Kebra Nagast* ranks among the world's greatest epic literature. It's not merely a collection of entertaining stories of legendary and historical heroes; the *Kebra Nagast* recounts and expresses the dreams and memories, the thoughts, feelings, and actions of an entire nation. Viewed in this context, the *Kebra Nagast* could be compared to Homer's two legendary works, *The Iliad* and *The Odyssey. Beowulf* and *Epic of Gilgamesh* also come to mind. All of these works summarize and express the nature and ideals of a people at a crucial period in their history.

However, for Ethiopian Christians the *Kebra Nagast* is not merely a literary work. Like the Hebrew *Bible* for the Jews and the *Koran* for the Arabs, the *Kebra Nagast* is a sacred text and the repository of Ethiopian national and religious feelings. Moreover, it is perhaps the truest and most genuine expression of Abyssinian Christianity, which has been woven into the fabric of Ethiopian life in the most intimate way.

The *Kebra Nagast* is regarded as the ultimate authority on the history of the Ethiopian people's conversion from pagan worship. Accordingly, it is considered to contain the final proof that (1) they are the true descendants of the Hebrew Patriarchs; (2) that the lawful kings of Ethiopia were descended from Solomon, king of Israel; and (3) that the Ark of the Covenant was brought from Jerusalem to Ethiopia by Menelik I, said to be the first-born son of Solomon.

This last point is of supreme importance, because not only was the Ark of the Covenant brought to Ethiopia, the Ethiopians claim that it has remained there to this day, its final resting place being St. Mary of Zion Church in Aksum, religious capital of Ethiopia. It is in a carefully guarded sanctuary of the church and always kept under wraps and seen by only one monk, who dedicates his life to watching over it. This has been the case for centuries. When one monk dies, another one is appointed to take his place.

Ethiopians regard this claim very seriously. "We are a people who defend itself not only by force of arms, but also by the authority of its writing, and upon its tradition and history reside the strength of the Kingdom," said one spokesman. And for the people "of the Kingdom" there's no greater written authority than the *Kebra Nagast*. This sacred text is a constant reminder that they are "the custodians of God's Covenant through the

Cathedral, Aksum, c. 1930 *This photograph is of the Mariam Cathedral (St. Mary of Zion). Only the building foundations are ancient. Here most Ethiopian emperors were crowned. As late as the 1930s the coronation jewels, hidden by priests from invaders for centuries, still could be viewed. Included in the church treasury were crowns and scepters dating back many centuries, including the gold crown of Emperor Fasil, or Fasiladas (1632–1667). The gold in some of these crowns, including the tall crown used by Menelik II at his 1889 coronation, dates back to the fourth century. Tradition is that the gold originally came from the unlocated mines of Ophir.*

The Ethiopian Orthodox Church traces its history to the second century. It is one of the oldest Christian sects in the world. Throughout the centuries, the church had played a dominant role in the politics and culture of Ethiopia. More than half of all Ethiopians are Christians, with their core area being the central Highlands. They predominate among the Amhara and Tegray people, but their influence is felt throughout the country.

treasure that it has bestowed" upon them. As mentioned earlier, it teaches that the lawful kings of Ethiopia were descended from Solomon, king of Israel; that the Tabernacle of the Law of God, the Ark of the Covenant, was brought from Jerusalem to Aksum by Menelik I, Solomon's first-born son; and that the

God of Israel transferred His place of abode on earth from Jerusalem to Ethiopia.

The central story of the *Kebra Nagast* is the legend of the queen of Sheba, also known to the Ethiopian people as Queen Makeda. According to the legend the queen possessed great wealth and beauty, and she had accomplished many great things during her reign. But she still was not satisfied. She felt that something was missing from her life.

The head of the queen's royal caravan was a man named Tamrin. One day, upon his return journey, he brought the queen a marvelous tale about a rich and powerful king who possessed great wisdom. His name was Solomon, and he was the king of Israel. The more the queen heard, the more she longed to travel to Jerusalem. One day she announced that she intended to travel to Jerusalem to see for herself this wise King Solomon.

Arriving in Jerusalem with a great caravan of almost eight hundred camels carrying large quantities of gold, spices, and precious stones, she was escorted to the palace of Solomon and talked with him about all that she had on her mind. The king answered all of her questions. Nothing was too difficult for him to explain, no matter what challenge she posed for him. When the queen heard the wisdom of Solomon and saw the palace he had built, the food on his table, the seating of his officials, the attending servants in their robes, his cupbearers, and the burnt offerings he made at the Temple of the Lord, she was over-whelmed. She said to the king, "The report I heard in my own country about your achievements and your wisdom is true. But I did not believe these things until I came and saw with my own eyes. Indeed, not even half was told to me. In wisdom and wealth you have far exceeded the report I heard."

During her six-month visit, the queen conferred frequently with King Solomon. She was so impressed with his wisdom that she gave up her religion and converted to Judaism. King Solomon was also impressed by the queen's beauty and intelli-gence, so much so that he desired to father many sons with her, sons who would rule in the name of Israel.

One night, after they consummated their relationship, Solomon had a dream that the sun had departed from Israel and shone brilliant over Ethiopia forever. Shortly thereafter, the queen returned to her own country laden with gifts from the king. He had also given her a ring as a token of remembrance. Nine months and five days later the queen of Sheba gave birth to a son. His royal name was Menelik, meaning "the son of the wise man."

When Menelik was growing up he showed great curiosity as to the identity of his father, but the queen kept the secret hidden until she thought the time was right. She feared that her son would depart and be lost to her forever. When her son was twenty-two she revealed the truth, and Menelik made preparations to depart to Jerusalem to visit his father. His mother gave him the ring Solomon had given her all those many years ago, as proof of his identity. She also gave him a letter in which she requested that Solomon send her part of the cover of the Ark of the Covenant so that it might be venerated in her country.

When Menelik arrived at his father's court, he didn't need the ring his mother gave him. Everyone was astonished at Menelik's resemblance to the king. When he finally reached his father, Solomon stated, "He's handsomer than I am, and his form and stature are those of David, my father, in his early manhood."

Solomon kissed and embraced his son and asked him to stay. He promised Menelik the kingdom of Israel upon his death, but Menelik replied, "My Lord, it's impossible for me to abandon my mother. I swore to her that I would return."

While in Jerusalem Menelik studied the laws and institutions of the Hebrews, but he decided to return home. When Solomon realized that he couldn't persuade his son to remain, he had the priest anoint Menelik king of Ethiopia and bestowed upon him the name of David. He summoned the elders of Israel and commanded them to send their first-born sons with Menelik for the founding of Israel's new kingdom in Ethiopia.

Before the young men departed from Jerusalem, they abducted the Ark of the Covenant and carried it with them to Ethiopia. The divine presence had now left Jerusalem and settled over the capital of Ethiopia.

When Menelik and his entourage reached his mother's country, the queen was waiting to receive him and the Ark of the Covenant. There was great rejoicing, and the queen abdicated her throne in favor of her son. From that time forward, the people abandoned their worship of idols and accepted the God of the Hebrews, and Menelik and his descendants sat on the throne of Ethiopia. Except for brief periods, the descendants of the queen of Sheba and Solomon, king of Israel, ruled the throne of Ethiopia. Emperor Haile Selassie I was the last lawful king descended from the House of David.

The *Kebra Nagast* provides an explanation for three recurring themes that are intricately woven throughout the history of Ethiopia. In summary, these themes are (1) the descent of the royal family, (2) the presence of the Ark of the Covenant as proof of the sanctity of the Ethiopian state, and (3) the validity of the belief that the people of Ethiopia are the chosen people.

Many historians dispute the accuracy of the story presented in the *Kebra Nagast*. Some claim that Menelik was not a historical figure, but rather a legendary character like Achilles and Odysseus from Greek mythology. Several authorities also suggest that in Solomon's time, a thousand years before Christ, Ethiopia had not possessed any real civilization capable of producing so illustrious a monarch as the queen of Sheba.

In spite of these doubts, there seems to be a general agreement among Ethiopians that the Ark of the Covenant did eventually end up in their country and remains there to this day. They point to at least one other source as justification for their claim.

This other source comes in the form of a document, *Churches and Monasteries of Egypt and Some Neighbouring Countries,* written by a twelfth-century Armenian geographer named Abu Salih. In a chapter entitled "Abyssinia," (a term commonly used to refer to Ethiopia), Salih makes the following observation: "The Abyssinians possess the Ark of the Covenant, in which are two tables of stone inscribed by the finger of God with the commandments which he ordained for the Children of Israel. The Ark of the Covenant is placed upon the altar, but is not so wide as the altar. It is as high as the knee of a man and is overlaid with gold."

Equally important is the detailed account Abu Salih writes about how the Ark of the Covenant is treated with a sense of reverence by the Ethiopian people. "The Liturgy is celebrated upon the Ark four times in the year, within the palace of the king; and a canopy is spread over it when it is taken out from its own church to the palace of the King."

This description sounds remarkably like processions that still take place in Ethiopia today. One in particular is called the Timkat Festival, or Feast of the Epiphany. It is an annual celebration that takes place on the 19th of January, two weeks after the Ethiopian Christmas, and commemorates the baptism of Christ in the Jordan River.

Timkat celebrations begin with church–led processions and all-night prayer vigils. On Timkat Eve, priests remove the *tabot,* symbol of the Ark of the Covenant, from their churches and carry it in a procession, making sure it is covered with ornate cloth at all times. Priests carrying sacred relics such as Bibles, crosses, and silver canes lead the processions. It is this tradition of profound spirituality that is the key to understanding the nature of Ethiopia's claim to be the final resting place of the Ark of the Covenant. According to one of the priests who leads the annual Timkat procession, "The Ark is central to our faith. It is testimony to our religion."

Cotton Market, Gidami, 1900   *Cotton is grown in the fertile Awash River valley of eastern Ethiopia. In this area, sugar and cotton are the major cash crops.*

2

TRIALS, TRIBULATIONS, AND TRIUMPHS

Now Poseidon had gone off to the Ethiopians, who are at the world's end, and lie in two halves, the one looking West and the other East. He had gone there to accept a hecatomb of sheep and oxen, and was enjoying himself at his festival.

Homer/*The Odyssey*

Ethiopia is a mountainous country located in the Horn of Africa. The "Horn" of Africa, named for its shape, juts out along the Red Sea into the Indian Ocean, just south of the Arabian Peninsula. Occupying an area of 437,600 square miles, Ethiopia is larger than Texas, Oklahoma, and New Mexico combined. Ethiopia is a landlocked country, roughly the shape of a pyramid or triangle. It's bordered on all sides by independent African countries or territories. On its northern border is Eritrea, a country that gained its independence from Ethiopia in 1993. Djibouti lies to the east, Sudan to the west, and Kenya and Somalia to the south and southeast.

Ethiopia has natural splendor of startling majesty. Astonishing desert scenes give way to expansive views of the Red Sea. Mountain vistas of staggering beauty descend with breathtaking rapture into lovely, lazy lakes that dot the countryside. Lake Tana,

Water Carriers, Massawa, 1901 *The Eritrean port city of Massawa is one of the world's hottest places, with an annual average temperature of 86 degrees Fahrenheit. The city was badly destroyed in 1990 during the war for Eritrean independence. Most of the inhabitants are Muslim. Population (1992 estimate) 40,000*

the Blue Nile River, and ancient cities like Aksum and Gondar are just part of the ethereal charm that add elements of mystery and intrigue to the geographical landscape known as Ethiopia.

Apart from its natural splendor, Ethiopia is also the home of our earliest human ancestors. In November 1994 Yohannes Haile Selassie, an Ethiopian scientist trained in the United States, discovered near Aramis on Ethiopia's Awash River, a group of handlike bones approximately 4.4 million years old. Not long after this discovery, other anthropologists working near the same site found additional bones and reconstructed almost an entire skeleton.

Crossing the Omo River, c. 1900   *The Omo River in southern Ethiopia flows south into Lake Rudolf near the Kenya border. The Omo River region is rich in early fossil remains. The layers of volcanic ash, which scientists can date, reveal that the area, now an arid wasteland, was once a fertile region with several rivers and lush forests.*

In 1967 a group of paleoanthropologists led by Richard Leakey recovered parts of two skulls and a number of limb bones from sites along the Omo River. These fragments have been dated to the East African Late Middle Pleistocene or Early Late Pleistocene (about two hundred to seventy thousand years ago). This discovery is regarded as an excellent early example of the African segment of evolving Homo sapiens.

In January 1995 the scientists announced their discovery to the world. They had discovered the world's oldest known human ancestor. They named their discovery *Australopithecus ramidus*— *Australopithecus*, meaning "Southern Ape," and *ramidus,* a word in local Afar language meaning "root," or "ancestry."

Twenty years earlier, the skeletal remains of the second oldest ancestors was also found in Ethiopia. Known internationally as Lucy, after the Beatles' song "Lucy in the Sky with Diamonds," this skeleton is approximately 3.2 million years old. Her scientific name is *Australopithecus afarensis*. The first of these words, as you'll recall, means "Southern Ape"; the second alludes to the Afar region where she was discovered. However, the people of Ethiopia simply refer to Lucy as *Denqenesh*, meaning, "She is wonderful."

Apart from its majestic beauty, Ethiopia has long been regarded as a land of legend, a land shrouded in myth and mystery. As a result, it has held a special fascination for people in other countries, a fascination stemming from images created and exported by writers and travelers. These images, according to some historians, derive from a variety of sources. Some relate to the legends associated with the claim that Ethiopian kings are descendants of the Lion of Judah, and that Ethiopia is the final resting place of the Ark of the Covenant. Others are associated with stories of Prester John, the legendary Christian king and priest. The first record of Prester John appears in the writings of a German bishop and historian named Otto Freising. It was generally believed that the kingdom of Prester John was located in Africa, where it was frequently identified with the Christian kingdom of Abyssinia. The term Abyssinia is of Arabic origin. It comes from the Arabic word *Habash,* the name of one of the first Ethiopian groups that Arabs came in contact with. This was the name they gave the entire country. The survival of Ethiopia's Orthodox Christianity, the strength of its cultural, linguistic, and religious institutions, and Ethiopia's unrelenting struggle for independence in the midst of a continent under constant assault and domination by European powers, has also been a remarkable source of inspiration for legends and stories about this extraordinary country and its people.

Afar People, Asseb, c. 1901 *The Afar (Arabic:* Denakil*) are a Muslim nomadic people who live in the northeastern corner of Ethiopia, a terrifying area of volcanic ruins, stark saline cliffs, lava, dried lakes, and merciless desert. "[It is] a landscape of terror, of hardship, of death," wrote explorer L. M. Nesbitt, among the first Europeans to travel in the region.*

The Afar are a Hamitic people who have lived here for centuries and who are linked by legend to the biblical sons of Ham. Their subsistence economy depends on livestock, especially goats, some camels, and, more rarely, cattle.

This photograph was taken by L. Naretti, an Italian professional photographer who lived in Massawa.

Afar People, c. 1895   *The Afar (Arabic: Denakil) are one of the most primitive peoples living in Ethiopia. They live in the northeastern corner of the country. The wandering Afar are usually not friendly to strangers—for one more person means less water for everyone in this blindingly hot area with temperatures higher than 120 degrees Fahrenheit. The Afar men almost always carry either a spear or a broad-bladed knife, as they traditionally divide their time between herding and fighting either with each other or with neighboring tribes. Unfortunately, the lack of rainfall in what is called the Denakil Depression has created an unprecedented famine in this area in recent years.*

Many of these legends are captured in the *Kebra Nagast*, the sacred text of the Ethiopian people. But according to Richard Pankhurst in his book *The Ethiopians: A History,* Ethiopia's first recorded contact was with Egypt during the time of the pharaohs. Egyptian inscriptions refer to the southern Red Sea coast as the Land of Punt. Punt has been identified with territory on both the Arabian and African coasts. The cargo that the Egyptians obtained from Punt, notably gold and ivory, suggests however,

Nobleman, Aksum, c. 1900   *Aksum (Axum) was a powerful kingdom in northern Ethiopia during the early Christian era. In the vicinity of Aksum, archaeologists have found an ancient Himyaritic temple—identified by seven inscriptions. The Himyarites are mentioned by the Roman writer Pliny in the latter half of the first century. The Aksum kingdom reached its height in East Africa between the 300s and the 600s. It occupied land that is now Eritrea, northern Ethiopia, and parts of the Sudan. Aksum grew rich and powerful because of Adulis, its port on the Red Sea. Adulis, near today's city of Massawa, was a major trading city for gold and ivory. These precious goods were traded to Egypt, Greece, Rome, Persia, and India. At its peak, the Aksumite kings built impressive fortresses, palaces, and granite monuments. Some of these granite obelisks still stand in Aksum. During the 600s Muslims eventually surrounded the Christians of Aksum, and Aksum then lost power and territory. What survived of its culture became integrated into what we now call Ethiopia.*

that these were primarily of African origin. The gold was probably from the Ethiopian interior. The ivory was from elephants that inhabited the coast as well as the interior of Africa.

Again according to Pankhurst, contacts first with the Land of Punt, and later with Ophir and the elephant-hunting grounds, did much to shape the ancient world's image of Ethiopia. The Greeks who first gave the country its name, the Land of Burnt Faces, regarded it with awe, both as a far-off realm and as a land inhabited by remarkable people.

In his epic poem *The Odyssey,* Homer describes the Ethiopians as *eschatoi andron*, "the most distant of Men." He writes that they lived "at earth's two verges, in sunset lands and lands of the rising sun." The Ethiopians were regarded by the Greeks as the best people in the world. Homer writes of them in *The Iliad* as the "blameless Ethiopians." He claims that Zeus, the king of gods, visited them; that the goddess of the rainbow, Iris, traveled to their country to participate in their sacrificial rites; and that Poseidon, the sea god, lingered, delighted, at Ethiopian feasts.

Ethiopia is also frequently mentioned in the Bible. The Book of Zephaniah and the Book of Isaiah both echo the ancient Greeks in describing the country as a far-off place, as suggested by the phrase "beyond the rivers of Ethiopia." Reference to Ethiopia is also found in Genesis, which speaks of the river Gyon, "which compasseth the whole of Ethiopia," and in the Book of Numbers, which states that Moses married an Ethiopian woman. But perhaps the most important biblical reference, one that is a central theme in the *Kebra Nagast,* comes from Psalm 68:31. It prophesies, "Ethiopia shall soon stretch out her hands unto God."

In the twentieth century, Pan-Africanists and scholars like W.E.B. DuBois saw Ethiopia as the mother to all men, an ancient land of immense importance to human history. At the same time, the followers of Marcus Garvey and later the Rastafarians envisioned Ethiopia as a spiritual homeland. They dreamed that some day the children of slaves might return to Africa and live in Ethiopia, a nation that, as stated in the book of Psalms, stretched out her hands unto God.

Granite Column, Aksum, c. 1929 *This solid granite column at Aksum poses a riddle. Archaeologists believe pagan artisans carved the stele before Ethiopia was Christianized—but they cannot explain how the solid block was quarried. A nonfunctional door and windows resemble the southern Arabian earthen skyscrapers. This seventy-feet-tall column may mark the site of an unexcavated royal tomb.*

In more recent times, television and newspapers have depicted Ethiopia in harsh terms as a land engulfed in the perpetual turmoil of war, famine, and revolution. It seems that despite the fascination Ethiopia has held for many people over the centuries, knowledge about the realities of its political, social, and economic affairs has become limited and often fragmentary. It seems that knowledge of Egypt's legendary and glorious past has slipped from the world's memory.

Modern Ethiopia traces its origins to the ancient kingdom of Aksum, one of Africa's most important cultural and trading

Ethiopian Orthodox, Priest, Lekempti, c. 1900 *The Ethiopian Orthodox Church is an independent Christian church headquartered in Addis Ababa. Its ancient religion has been preserved virtually intact since the fifth century. It holds to a monophysite doctrine— which means that Christ's nature remains divine and never human even though He has taken on a human body with its cycle of birth, life, and death. The liturgy is celebrated in the ancient Ethiopian Ge'ez language (from which Amharic is derived).*

The Ethiopian Orthodox Church is headed by the abuna *(Arabic: "Our Father"). The* abuna *presides over numerous churches and many richly endowed monasteries. It is estimated that the Church owned at least one fifth of the arable land before the 1974 revolution. Approximately 20 percent of all Christian males are either priests or in some religious order. Priests are expected to marry, only monks and nuns are celibate.*

centers. Migrants from southern Arabia were one of the most significant influences on the development of the early Aksumite Kingdom. They arrived a thousand years before the birth of Christ, bringing with them Semitic speech, writing, and a distinctive stone-building architecture. The kingdom became a thriving center in which merchants from various parts of the ancient world came together to exchange gold and ivory, cloth, glassware, tools, and other items they thought precious.

Christianity became the state religion in the Aksumite Kingdom in the fourth century during the reign of King Ezana. He founded the first Christian Orthodox Church in Ethiopia, which was deeply influenced by the Coptic Church, or Christian Church of Egypt. This single event has continued to shape and influence the lives of the Ethiopian people into the present millennium. Few African countries have had such a long, varied, and troubled past as Ethiopia, and yet in spite of turmoil and upheavals, the founding of the Ethiopian Orthodox church remains an event of supreme importance. It is one of the longest living institutions in the history of Ethiopia. Both spiritually and symbolically it represents the faith and hope, dreams and memories, thoughts, feelings, and actions of an entire nation.

However, even though Christianity became the state religion it was not and is not the only religion practiced. One of the most remarkable aspects of Ethiopia is its cultural diversity. In fact, it can be argued that no single Ethiopian culture exists. Rather, many different cultural, ethnic, religious, and linguistic groups exist within Ethiopia. It's estimated that the country is home to more than one hundred different ethnic groups, the largest of which are the Oromo, Amhara, Tegray, and Somali. More than seventy different languages are spoken in the country. Ethiopia's diversity has greatly enriched the country over the centuries, but it has also led to conflict.

This is especially true of Ethiopian Jews, an ethnic group of northwestern Ethiopia that practiced a form of Judaism. Outsiders often referred to Ethiopian Jews as *Falasha,* meaning "stranger" or "gone into exile." However, the community considered the term derogatory and preferred instead *Beta Israel*, a Hebrew term meaning "House of Israel." Although the origins

Oromo People, c. 1900   *Early in the sixteenth century the Oromo (Galla) immigration from the Somali Plain profoundly changed Ethiopian history. In successive waves onto the main Ethiopian plateau, the Oromo came, adopting local customs and intermarrying to such an extent that their original culture is lost.*

The Oromo live mainly in the western, southern, and eastern parts of Ethiopia. They are divided into many tribes, the major ones being Arusi, Sidamo, Tegray, Afar, Sano, and Agew. Together, they constitute about one third of the peoples of Ethiopia. This photograph, and the following three, capture the various faces of the divergent Oromo people.

Oromo People, c. 1900

Oromo People, c. 1900

Oromo People, c. 1900

of Judaism in Ethiopia remain a mystery, scholars suggest the community's roots extend 2,500 years. Some of *Beta Israel* believe that they are descendants of Menelik, the son of Solomon and Sheba, thus giving more credence to the story of the Ark of the Covenant presented in the *Kebra Nagast*.

When the kingdom of Aksum adopted Christianity as its official religion, the Beta Israel was forced to relocate to the mountainous region around Lake Tana. Over the centuries they gradually gave up their land and Agaw language and adopted many of the customs and language of their Amhara neighbors.

Judaism was not the only challenger to Christianity in the Aksumite Empire. Early in the seventh century a new religion called Islam was founded by the Prophet Muhammad in what is now Saudi Arabia, across the Red Sea from Ethiopia. When Muslims, the followers of Muhammad, were persecuted in Arabia, Muhammad advised them to flee to Ethiopia. Initially, Ethiopian Christians welcomed them, but as more and more Muslims escaped into the coastal regions, they came into conflict with the Christians. Continued conflict and warfare disrupted the trade and cultural life the people of Ethiopia had maintained for centuries. This is one of the reasons why the Aksumite Kingdom declined. Because of the breakdown of the Red Sea trade, Ethiopia's political power shifted, and the country began a new and tumultuous period in its history.

For centuries Ethiopia had been ruled by a monarchy guided by the doctrines of Christianity. This arrangement provided a sense of continuity and stability; as a result, the country and its people prospered. But with the fall of the Akssumite Kingdom this prosperity ended. So did the country's cherished heritage of being the first and only Christian country in Africa. The royal lineage that could be traced back to Menelik I, and through him to King Solomon and the House of David, was broken for the first time. A time of trials and tribulations followed.

It was a time in which numerous ethnic groups and individuals competed for power. According to the Ethiopian tradition, one of these individuals was a tribal queen named Gudit, who adhered to the Jewish faith and seemed to have been motivated by the sole purpose to obliterate the Christian religion. Even though it was no longer the symbol it once was, she attacked Aksum, and burnt and pillaged much of the ancient city, destroying many churches and other Christian symbols. According to the tradition Gudit was the final straw that broke the back of an already falling kingdom. Gudit was the queen of the Agaw, to which the Falashas, the Ethiopian Jews, also belonged. Although it's not certain that she left any direct successor, historians believe that within fifty years of her death the majority of northern Ethiopia united under the Zagwe Monarch.

The Zagwe period extended from about A.D. 1137 to 1270. Their capital was at Roha, later renamed Lalibala after King Lalibala, the most notable ruler of the Zagwe Dynasty. He is renowned for building eleven churches that were carved out of existing rock in the city that bears his name. These famous rock-hewn churches are still used today, nearly a thousand years after they were created. They have even been described as the eighth wonder of the world.

In spite of its achievements, the Zagwe Dynasty clashed with other groups, especially the ones who wanted the descendants of Solomon and the queen of Sheba to rule Ethiopia once again. During the fifty years following Lalibala's death in 1220, the Zagwe were constantly at war. In 1270 Yekuno Amalak, a king claiming to be of the Solomonic line, ascended the throne. His ascension brought an end to the Zagwe Dynasty.

The restoration of the Solomonic Dynasty marked a turning point in Ethiopian history. The center of political power, for the next two hundred and fifty years, was firmly established in Shoa, and the influence and wealth of the church was strengthened. The church became a major landowner.

Although Yekuno Amalak once again brought honor to the house of Sheba, it was his grandson, Emperor Amda Seyon (1314–1344), who consolidated the power of the royal family. Through several victorious campaigns he created a powerful state throughout central Ethiopia. But it was Amalak's great-grandson, Zara Xaqob (1432–1468), who brought the new dynasty into full bloom. He was considered the greatest Ethiopian ruler since King Ezana.

During the reign of the Solomonic emperors the country witnessed a flowering of Ethiopian literature. Besides the *Kebra Nagast*, with its legendary story of the queen of Sheba's visit to Solomon, the country's first real history was written during this period. This was the first series of *Royal Chronicles* written for the Solomonic emperors down to modern times. They provide a chronological narrative of the entire period. An equally significant document produced during this time was the *Fetha Nagast*, or *Laws of the Kings*. Written in the ancient Ge'ez language, it

Royal Throne, Aksum, c. 1930   *This stone throne and four pillars date to the first to fourth centuries. Aksum, from its base on the Tegray Plateau, controlled the ivory trade between the Sudan and the port of Adulis on the Red Sea. (The inland city of Aksum was about a five-day march from Adulis.) The people spoke Ge'ez, a Semitic language. In the 600s, Aksum's power fell sharply as the Muslims gained control of Arabia, the Red Sea, and the coast of northern Africa. The Muslims, enemies of the Christian Aksums, ended the kingdom's foreign trade. It is believed that this stone was the throne of the ancient Aksum rulers.*

provided Ethiopia with its principal legal code. This code was consulted by Ethiopian monarchs when giving judgment and remained in use until the early twentieth century.

Because of these and other achievements, the new Solomonic Dynasty regained the power and prestige it had lost over a century earlier. The country was poised on the brink of its most important epoch.

Ethiopian Military Officer with His Four Slaves, 1899 *In November 1889 an international antislavery conference convened in Brussels. The major powers of the world agreed to save the "oppressed and decimated" races of Africa by using their prestige and authority to both end slavery and the "monstrous trade in human flesh." Emperor Menelik II (1889–1913) accepted the conference's resolutions and promised to implement them at once. But slavery and the slave trade continued in Ethiopia without any changes for many more years.*

3

THE STRUGGLE FOR INDEPENDENCE

The oppressor never voluntarily gives freedom. It must be demanded by the oppressed.

Martin Luther King, Jr. (1929–1968)

For almost three centuries after the Solomonic Dynasty came to power, Ethiopia engaged in a protracted struggle with the followers of Islam. Conflict between the *cross* and the *crescent* was not an uncommon event in Ethiopia. It had been going on since the followers of Muhammad first crossed the borders of Ethiopia, fleeing persecution in Saudi Arabia. But this time the circumstances were different. This time the Muslim invaders were not just looking for sanctuary within the borders of Ethiopia. This time they came prepared for war. As a result, the stakes were higher and the consequences more profound. And as if these circumstances were not severe enough, there was a storm gathering on the horizon that would shake the country to its very foundation. Whether the people of Ethiopia knew it or not, they were poised on the brink of another major turning point in their history. But first things first.

From the end of the fifteenth century until the reign of Tewodros II, who came to power in 1855, an atmosphere of anarchy and chaos settled over Ethiopia. The country witnessed an intensification of the old struggle between the Christian kingdom and its Muslim neighbors. The conflict intensified even more when the Muslims were unified under the charismatic leadership of an able warrior named Mahfuz. Mahfuz adopted the title *Imam,* an Islamic term used to designate the descendents of the Prophet Mohammad. The title was significant because it justified Mahfuz's claim to be a religious leader; therefore, his raids against the Christians were not simply acts of aggression but *jihad,* or Holy War. He declared that a jihad is no hardship for Muslims. "Whoever of us is killed will go to paradise, and whoever survives will enjoy happiness."

Mahfuz's invasions occurred at a time when international developments were taking place in the Red Sea region. Two of the world's colonial powers, Portugal and the Ottoman Empire, had established colonies in the area. The Portuguese seized the east African port of Kilwa on the Indian Ocean coast, south of Ethiopia, and the eastern mouth of the Red Sea. The Ottoman Empire invaded Egypt and Yemen and began extending its influence on the Mediterranean and Rea Sea coasts. Seeking to expel the Portuguese from the Indian Ocean, the Ottomans created a naval fleet at Suez, Egypt.

The appearance of two colonial powers, one Christian and one Muslim, each bent on exclusive domination of the region, was destined to have a profound impact on Ethiopia. Up to this point Ethiopia had been preoccupied with its own internal struggles and had remained largely isolated from international affairs. But now, all of a sudden, the nation was forced to pay attention to such affairs and make up for lost time.

The hostility between Portugal and the Ottoman Empire dated back to 1497. In that year Portuguese navigator Vasco da Gama sailed around the Cape of Good Hope, at the southern tip of Africa, and in the spring of 1498 became the first European to reach India by sea route. This voyage inaugurated a lucrative spice trade between Europe and South Asia. As a result, Portuguese fleets began to shut down Arab shipping routes between India, southern Arabia, and Egypt that supplied the Ottoman spice trade. But at the same time the conflict between Portugal and the Ottoman Empire had its personal element. When asked what brought him from Portugal on such a hazardous journey, da Gama is reported to have answered, *"Christians and spices."* In fact, when Vasco da Gama set off on his famous voyage he was carrying two things, a white silk banner with the double red cross of the Order of Christ embroidered upon it, and letters of Credence for delivery to Prester John.

Also, although his ultimate destination was indeed India, the Portuguese explorer devoted a considerable part of the expedition to African exploration and is reported to have wept for joy when, at anchor off Mozambique, he was told that Prester John lived in the interior far to the north. It has been suggested that da Gama's subsequent stopovers at Malindi, Mombasa, Brava (where he built a lighthouse that still stands), and Mogadishu were in part motivated by his continuing desire to make contact with Prester John.

Though in its isolation and preoccupation with its own affairs, Ethiopia had seemingly lost interest in the world beyond its immediate borders, that world had certainly not lost interest in Ethiopia. It was still the fabled home of the Ark of the Covenant and the land of the legendary Prester John. And that world, without waiting to be extended a special invitation, had suddenly and irrevocably arrived on Ethiopia's doorstep.

With the *"world"* standing uninvited at its door, Ethiopia still had to contend with Mahfuz and his Holy War. Mahfuz undertook no less than twenty-five annual raids into the Christian highlands of Shawa, Amhara, and Fatagar. These were generally carried out during Lent, just prior to the Easter feast. In the course of these campaigns the victorious Muslims carried off numerous slaves and livestock and generally disrupted the peace and continuity of the country.

Mahfuz's Holy War was brought to an abrupt end during the reign of Lebna Dengel, who had assumed the throne at age twelve after the death of his father. His mother, Empress Eleni, ruled the country in his place. During a final confrontation between the two opposing forces, Mahfuz challenged any

Amhara Children, 1929 *The Amhara are one of the two largest linguistic groups in Ethiopia, the other being the Oromo. They constitute about one third of the nation's population and have dominated its history. Amharic was the official language until the 1990s. Along with the Tegray people, the Amhara are the principal adherents of the Ethiopian Orthodox Church.*

Christian to a duel to the death. A monk called Gabra Endreyas accepted the challenge. A fierce contest ensued that ended with the death of Mahfuz. Deprived of their leader, Mahfuz's soldiers deserted the battlefield.

Although Mahfuz's death brought an end to the reign of terror, the Christians of Ethiopia were not out of danger. In fact, they had not yet faced their worst enemy. His name was Imam Ahmad ibn Ibrahim, but the Christians of Ethiopia called him *Gragn,* "the left-handed." Not since Queen Gudit had they faced such a dreaded enemy.

During the course of these developments two Portuguese ambassadors, Fernao Gomes and Joao Sanchez, arrived in

Ethiopia from the East African coast of Malindi. Fearing further conflict with the Muslims, Empress Eleni formed an alliance with the Portuguese, and they remained in Ethiopia for six years. During this time Lebna Dengel came of age and assumed his rightful place on the throne. Unlike Empress Eleni, the young emperor was reluctant to continue an alliance with the Portuguese even though the Muslims under the leadership of Gragn posed a constant threat. After a while all ties were severed, and the Portuguese departed the country. During the years that the they had remained in Ethiopia a chaplain, Francisco Alvares, wrote the first detailed description of the country, *The Verdadera Informacam das terras do Preste Joam,* or *The Truthful Information about the Countries of Prester John.* Throughout this document Alvarez referred to the emperor of Ethiopia as *"Prester"* or *"Prester John."* Alverez was the first European to document the Ethiopian version of the legend of the queen of Sheba and the birth of her son Menelik.

With the departure of the Portuguese, Gragn mounted his Holy War. His troops swept through Ethiopia, destroyed churches and monasteries, and forcibly converted much of the population to Islam. Confronted with the overwhelming forces of Gragn's armies, Lebna Dengel fled to the mountaintop monastery at Debra Damo. Faced with certain defeat, Lebna Dengel recanted his earlier position toward the Portuguese and requested their assistance in defeating Gragn. The Portuguese dispatched a well-armed force of four hundred handpicked men led by Christopher da Gama, the son of the famous explorer. By the time they arrived in Ethiopia, Lebna Dengel had died, but his son, Galawdewos, had succeeded him to the throne. With their combined efforts the two Christian forces defeated the Muslims at the battle of Wayna Daga. Gragn was killed, probably shot to death by a Portuguese musket, and his son, Muhammad, was taken prisoner. Thus, another attempt to defeat the Christian kingdom of Ethiopia was brought to a brutal end.

The protracted struggle between Gragn and the Christians of Ethiopia was one of the most traumatic events in the country's long history. It had taken considerable toll on the peace and security of the country. The Christian monarchy was virtually

Oromo Man with Berta Slave, c. 1900 *Slavery, which had existed in Ethiopia from time immemorial, was abolished by emperors Johannes IV (1872–1889) and Menelik II (1889–1913), but their decrees were ignored. In 1923, as a condition for membership in the League of Nations, Ethiopia had to promise to end slavery once and for all. Major abolition orders were promulgated in 1924 and 1931. Emperor Haile Selassie (1930–1974) implemented these orders with a sweeping decree. He emancipated children born to slave parents and slaves on their owners' deaths. But all of these decrees proved virtually impossible to enforce. Most officials ignored them.*

In 1932 Lord Noel Buxton met with Emperor Haile Selassie on behalf of great Britain's Anti-Slavery and Aborigines Protection Society. Again, the emperor agreed to end slavery—but this time, within twenty years. In 1934 the emperor created some sixty-two local bureaus to which he assigned judges who were instructed to free all slaves. Although this effort received publicity throughout the world, the work of the judges was negligible. Even westernized Ethiopians claimed that a sudden change ending slavery would create an economic upheaval. They argued that the liberated men and women could never fend for themselves. It was under Italian occupation (1936–1941) that slavery finally ended in Ethiopia.

Palace of Emperor Tewodros II, Magdala, 1868

destroyed. Many of its holiest and most beautifully decorated churches were in ruins. Only with the help of the Portuguese had the kingdom been able to survive. From this point forward Europeans would remain an intricate part of life in Ethiopia. The struggle against Gragn marked a turning point in the country's history. After his defeat, the country was impoverished. Many men, women, and children had been carried into slavery, and large numbers had been killed. Another outcome of the fighting was that large groups of people, especially the Oromo, began to migrate across Ethiopia. The country's sense of continuity and stability had been completely disrupted.

Royal Treasury (left), Magdala, 1868

Meanwhile, Spain and Portugal began to pressure the Christians of Ethiopia to abandon their Eastern Orthodox Religion and adopt Roman Catholicism. Initially, they had some success, but over time this acceptance turned into resistance and gradually turned into open rebellion. In fact, a civil war was fought along religious lines.

These events highlighted the fact that the emperors no longer exercised the authority that they once did. Regional provinces became more or less independent of each other, and more aggressive. The regional kings often fought each other for power. At one point there were six different men claiming the right to be the emperor of Ethiopia. This phase of Ethiopian history, which lasted until the reign of Tewodros II, was called the *"Age of the Princes"* because each region had its own supreme ruler, each vying for sole power of the kingdom. The country was waiting for the next strong emperor who would be able to unify the country again.

Sir Robert Napier (center), photographed with local troops and officials, Magdala, 1868

The first of these great rulers was Emperor Tewodros II, or Theodore, who has been called one of the most remarkable men in nineteenth-century Africa. Tewodros, whose birth name was Kasa Haylu, was born in 1818. His father was chief of a small western district on the border of the Sudan called Qwara. As a distant member of the royal family, he was brought up in a monastery, where he received an education and religious guidance, but he later became a freelance soldier. Tewodros began his rise to power during the *"Age of the Princes,"* but his ambition was different from those of the regional nobility. He wanted to establish a unified Ethiopian State and reform its administration and church. As a result of the loyalty he inspired in his supporters, he first became chief of Qwara and was duly crowned emperor in 1855. He chose the name Tewodros because of an Ethiopian legend that prophesied a monarch of that name would appear who would rule justly, defeat Islam, and capture Jerusalem. He didn't initially claim Solomonic lineage but did seek to restore the old Solomonic dynasty, and he considered himself the *"Elect of God."* Later, in an effort to add legitimacy

Heir Apparent of Emperor Tewodros II, Magdala, 1868 *For four years, 1868–1872, Ethiopia was plunged back into the old-time military battles between the feudal chieftains. The followers of Tewodros's eldest son and heir were unable to prevail. In 1872 the Ras (prince) of Tigre emerged triumphant from the struggle. He proclaimed himself Emperor Yohannes IV (1872–1889).*

Abyssinian Regiment, 1869

to his reign, he added "son of David and Solomon" to his title.

In an effort to unify the country and begin the task of modernization, Tewodros brought the various provinces under his control, reorganized the army, and raised taxes for its maintenance. He also made it illegal for his soldiers to steal from peasants. To strengthen his army he used the technical skills of Protestant missionaries to cast cannons and mortars. Also, with their help, he built the first roads in his country.

Tewodros's attempts at unification and modernization were overshadowed and ultimately brought to an abrupt end by a serious dispute with the British Government. Seeking aid from the British to enable him to consolidate his plans, Tewodros became unhappy with their response and had two British officials arrested. A well-equipped British Army stormed Tewodros' headquarters. Rather than face defeat or be captured, Tewodros committed suicide.

Ethiopian Soldiers, 1897 *The Battle of Adwa (1896) was a major event in Ethiopian history. Menelik II (1889–1913) suddenly became a world celebrity. Through this military victory, he ended the Italian government's assumption that Italy held a protectorate over Ethiopia. The Treaty of Addis Ababa (1896) between the king of Italy and the emperor of Ethiopia recognized the independence of Ethiopia. Subsequent treaties with Italy, France, and Great Britain fixed the borders of Ethiopia, with the neighboring territories ruled by the European powers.*

4

THE REIGN OF
MENELIK II

Many politicians of our time are in the habit of laying it down as a self-evident proposition that no people ought to be free till they are fit to use their freedom. The maxim is worthy of the fool in the old story who resolved not to go into the water until he had learnt to swim. If men are to wait for liberty till they become wise and good in slavery, they may indeed wait forever.

Thomas Babington Macaulay (1800–1859)

The next important nineteenth-century ruler was Emperor Yohannes IV, a chief from Tegray. The British, who gave him a large shipment of weapons as a reward for his neutrality during the conflict with Tewodros, assisted him in his rise to power. However, in spite of his reluctance to oppose the British, Yohannes was loyal to his country and a devout supporter of the Ethiopian Orthodox Church. He was the first ruler in modern times to achieve decisive victories against foreign enemies. The Egyptians, well-armed and trained by European and American officers, invaded Ethiopia twice during the 1870s. Both times, once in November 1875, at the battle of Gundet, and again in March 1876, at Gura, Yohannes defeated them. Later, in February 1885,

Oromo (Galla) Queen, 1868   *The queen of the Gallas (left) and her followers supported and assisted Sir Robert Napier in his march from Massawa to Magdala (1867–1868). This march was over mountains eight to ten thousand feet above sea level, which then descends into deep jungle, choked gorges, and ravines made virtually impassable by mud. Her son (standing) became Emperor Yohannes IV in 1872.*

the Italians, who were just beginning their colonial exploits, seized the port of Massawa. They were defeated at the battle of Dogali in January 1887.

In the last years of his reign, a group of Muslims known as the Mahdists attacked Ethiopia from the borders of the Sudan. Yohannes succeeded in defeating them at the Battle of Matamma in March 1889 but was killed by a sniper's bullet. Deprived of their emperor, Yohannes's army fled the battlefield. In the meantime, the Italians, taking advantage of the emperor's death, and of a serious famine that had recently broken out, invaded Ethiopia for the second time. In 1890 they established their Red Sea Colony of Eritrea. This set the stage for Ethiopia's first national hero of modern times.

Besides the struggle against invaders, the reign of Yohannes witnessed other important international developments that were destined to play a significant role in Ethiopia's history. For example, the opening of the Suez Canal in November 1869 greatly increased interest in the Red Sea area and the Gulf of Aden by colonial powers, especially the Italians, who were just beginning to look beyond their own borders with a desire of building a colonial empire. But more importantly, as far as Ethiopia was concerned, the opening of the Suez Canal helped to inaugurate a period in world history known as the *"Scramble for Africa."* This British term, coined in 1884, describes the twenty-odd years between the mid-1870s and 1902, when European powers explored, partitioned, and conquered nearly ninety percent of the African Continent. In the mid-1800s the European presence on the African continent was limited to coastal regions and a few interior areas in the south and east. In 1876, however, Belgium's King Leopold II announced his intent to explore the Congo, and in 1879 he sent Sir Henry Morgan Stanley into the area. In the same year the French began building a railway east from Dakar. That year also, France joined Great Britain in taking financial control of Egypt.

Tension between European powers seeking to add parts of Africa to their own colonial empire threatened to erupt into war.

In response, chancellor Otto von Bismarck of Germany convened the Berlin Conference of 1884–1885. Bismarck realized German interests might best be served by his taking control of the diplomatic struggles involving Africa. In addition, however, European powers recognized that rules and rationalizations were needed for the seizing of African territories, especially for territories that held potential for European conflict. Thus, the first phase of the scramble was largely a paper conquest conducted in the drawing rooms of European capitals. On the continent, though, explorers and soldiers such as Stanley, Pierre de Brazza, Frederick Lugard, and Cecil Rhodes acted as agents of European power, conquering weak African chiefs and signing treaties with the powerful ones.

In the early 1890s treaty-making gave way to conquest. Advances in military technology and medicine, especially the discovery of the anti-malarial agent "quinine," enabled Europeans to send troops into the heart of the continent. In half a generation France, Germany, Great Britain, Italy, Portugal, Spain, and King Leopold II of Belgium had acquired thirty new African colonies or protectorates covering 6 million square miles. A total of 110 million Africans had been divided into forty new political units, with some thirty percent of the borders drawn as straight lines, cutting through villages, ethnic groups, and African kingdoms. In Ethiopia Emperor Menelik II stood as an unmovable force against the advancing tide of colonialism.

Menelik was the third great nineteenth-century ruler of Ethiopia. From the beginning of his career he was inspired by Tewodros's dream of making Ethiopia a modern state. He sought to strengthen his army by befriending the European powers and importing large quantities of firearms. He was more successful with these goals than either one of his predecessors.

On the death of Yohannes, Menelik proclaimed himself emperor. To gain international recognition he signed a Treaty of Perpetual Peace and Friendship with the Italian government at the village of Wechale on May 2, 1889. The Wechale Treaty, as it is generally known, was written in Amharic and Italian and

Ras Mangasha c. 1890   *Ras (Prince) Mangasha of Tigre was the son of Emperor Yohannes IV (1872–1889). Emperor Yohannes IV spent most of his time repelling military threats from Egypt, Italy, and the fundamentalist Sudanese Mahdists. The Shewa ruler, Menelik II (1865–1889; later emperor, 1889–1913), ruled the historic kingdom of central Ethiopia and refused to recognize the authority of Yohannes IV.*

Finally, after years of warfare, in 1882 the two leaders acknowledged their separate spheres of influence. At the same time, in an attempt to create a greater Ethiopian empire in the future, they arranged a marriage between Yohannes IV's twelve-year-old son and Menelik II's seven-year-old daughter. The marriage contract also stipulated that Menelik would eventually succeed Yohannes IV as "king of kings" at some distant time.

Just prior to his death in 1889 Yohannes IV repudiated this agreement and announced that his eldest son, Ras Mangasha, would succeed him. Menelik, riding at the head of his Shewan troops and backed by Italy, crushed Ras Mangasha and his followers. These dynastic struggles paved the way for a united Ethiopia. Emperor Menelik (1889–1913) subsequently expanded Ethiopia's boundaries into areas never before under its rule. He modernized the new capital of Addis Ababa, opened elementary schools, built hospitals and hired foreign doctors, and established a national communications network. These projects were continued by Emperor Haile Selassie (1930–1974).

The success of Menelik and Haile Selassie in establishing a united Ethiopian kingdom convinced Italy's Benito Mussolini to undertake a preemptive strike before Ethiopia became strong enough to oppose Italian ambitions in the Horn of Africa. That action led to the Italo-Ethiopian War (1935).

contained clauses that benefited both countries. However, a dispute soon erupted over one of the clauses: Article 17. In Amharic it stated that Menelik *"could"* use the services of the government of the king of Italy when communicating with other governments or powers. The Italian text, on the other hand, stated that he *"must"* do so. The Italians used this latter text to claim that the agreement had given them a protectorate over Ethiopia. A protectorate would give Italy the final decision in all of Ethiopia's affairs. Menelik rejected this claim. To the king of Italy he wrote, "When I made the treaty I said that because of our friendship, our affairs in Europe might be carried out by the sovereign of Italy, but I have not made any treaty which obliges me to do so." Not long afterward, in February 1890, he wrote to the Great Powers, informing them that he did not accept the Italian interpretation of the agreement, and proudly declared, "Ethiopia has need of no one; she stretches out her hands to God."

In the meantime, the Italians occupied the northern highlands of Tegray. On January 1, 1890, they officially named their colony Eritrea, after the Latin term *Erythraeum Mare,* meaning "Red Sea." Once their colony was firmly entrenched, the Italians immediately began to expand, devouring more and more Ethiopian territory. They were encouraged in their ambitions by the British. In an effort to stabilize the regions and put a buffer between them and the Muslims of the Sudan, the British agreed with the Italian government that Ethiopia should fall within the Italian sphere of influence. France, on the other hand, encouraged Menelik to oppose the Italian threat by establishing boundaries of his empire. Anxious also to advance French economic interests through the construction of a new railroad, France reduced the size of its territorial claims and recognized Ethiopian sovereignty in the area.

Menelik meanwhile spent the next two years importing firearms. Most were purchased from France, Italy's colonial rival. Sizable gifts were also received from Russia, a fellow Eastern Orthodox country opposed to Catholic Italy. Thus strengthened militarily, and realizing that the Italians could not

Somali Caravan, Assab, c. 1900 *The nomadic Somali occupy all of Somalia, a strip of Djibouti, the southern Ethiopian region of Ogaden, and part of northwestern Kenya. It is believed that the Somali were converted to Islam in the fourteenth century by Arabs from across the Red Sea.*

Assab is a Red Sea port in southeastern Eritrea. Formerly a terminus of caravan routes across the Denakil Plain, the Assab coastal strip was acquired by Italian shipping interests in 1869. In 1885, it became the first Italian colonial possession in Africa.

be persuaded to abandon their Protectorate claim, Menelik finally decided to break off relations with Italy.

Likewise, it was clear to the Italians that they could not achieve their expansionist aims either by negotiations with Menelik or by subversion of local chiefs. As a result, the Italian Government concluded that its objectives could be achieved only by military action.

Mural in Church, Lekempti, 1900   *This mural in the Ethiopian Orthodox Church at Lekempti depicts the Battle of Adwa, or Adowa (March 1896) between the Ethiopian army of Menelik II (1889–1913) and Italian troops. The decisive Ethiopian victory checked Italy's attempt to build an African empire comparable to that of the French and British.*

In this mural the Italians, wearing helmets, are on the right, and the Ethiopians are on the left. At the far left is Menelik II, holding the Coptic cross of the Ethiopian Orthodox Church. The ignominy of this defeat was never forgotten in Italy. Writing to a young man bound for "the African War" in 1935, the author and political figure Gabriele D'Annunzio urged him to wipe out its memory he could still feel on his shoulders—"the scar, yes, the shameful scar, of Adowa."

Lekempti, not far from Adwa, is in north-central Ethiopia. In 1890 it was a thriving market town with a population of about 40,000. A European traveler wrote of it, "All kinds of produce, corn and honey being principal, and large quantities of cotton, native and American; iron and copper metal from the west are to be seen in the markets."

In late 1895 Italian forces invaded Tegray, just south of Eritrea. Menelik, learning that the Italian's had reached Dabra Hayla, mobilized against them. The two armies met at Adwa, in Tegray Province in northern Ethiopia, on March 1, 1896. The Ethiopians inflicted a crushing defeat on the Italians. Exact figures are not known, but it is estimated that about twelve thousand men died in the Battle of Adwa, the majority of them on the Italian side.

The Ethiopian victory at the Battle of Adwa in 1896 marked one of the first times that an African nation had defeated a European nation in a major battle. After this, Italy was forced to recognize Ethiopia's sovereignty. Had he done nothing else, Menelik would be remembered as Ethiopia's national hero for keeping his country independent at a time when Europeans were colonizing Africa. By the time the Ethiopians defeated the Italians, there were only two independent countries in Africa, Ethiopia and Liberia. All the others had been carved up among Great Britain, France, Germany, Portugal, Italy, Belgium, and Spain. Ethiopia would have certainly fallen under the gun if it had not been for the strength and ingenuity of the Ethiopian people and the country's first national hero, Menelik II, the two-hundredth-and-fifty-fourth descendant of the queen of Sheba and King Solomon.

The Jester of Emperor Menelik II, Addis Ababa, c.1900 *The court jester or fool was a source of amusement. Often dwarfs were kept for luck—that is, the belief that the deformed could avert "the evil eye," a glance that had the ability to cause misfortune or death. This elderly court jester appears to be less than four feet tall, slightly higher than a standard rifle.*

5

RAS TAFARI

Africa is a paradox which illustrates and highlights neo-colonialism. Her earth is rich, yet the products that come from above and below the soil continue to enrich, not Africans predominantly, but groups and individuals who operate to Africa's impoverishment.

Kwame Nkrumah (1900–1972)

Emperor Menelik II spent the final decade of his reign promoting modernization in Ethiopia. Along with his wife, Empress Taytu, he founded a new capital city, Addis Ababa, or "New Flower," a name chosen by Empress Taytu. It is still the capital of Ethiopia to this day. The new capital featured paved streets, hospitals, and secular schools. Menelik drove the first automobile in Ethiopia, and he founded government ministries like those of European nations and replaced hereditary territorial rulers with trained civil servants. He maintained an Ethiopian standing army, streamlined the tax system, created a national currency, imported the nation's first printing press, and promoted the use of telephones. In addition, Menelik commissioned a railway from Addis

Ababa to the seaport at Djibouti City, which a French firm completed in 1917, four years after the emperor's death.

Thus, modernization finally arrived on the doorsteps of the people of Ethiopia. The storm that had gathered on their horizon over a century before had brought terrible and drastic change. But even though this terrible storm had shaken the country to its very core, when the calm finally arrived it found the people of Ethiopia free, independent, and prepared to embrace their future, regardless of what that might bring. For the first time in recent memory, peace reigned in Africa's oldest Christian kingdom. Yet, Ethiopia was poised on the brink of yet another dramatic turning point in its history.

After serving as emperor for nearly twenty-five years, Menelik II died in December 1913, having named his grandson, Lij Iyasu, to succeed him. But the teenager was young and impetuous. In a country that had a long and proud Christian heritage, the young emperor showered favors on the Muslim community. Some historians suggest that Iyasu really wanted to create a nonsectarian Ethiopia, but all he succeeded in doing was alienating the nobility of Ethiopia, and with it the Ethiopian Orthodox Church. The young emperor also made the mistake, during the First World War, of befriending the Germans, Austrians, and the Ottoman Empire. As a result, he lost the support of the Allied Powers, Italy, France, and Great Britain. Leaders of the church, the army, and the country's nobility overthrew Iyasu. He had little option but to flee into the Afar lowlands, where he found asylum with supporters sympathetic to his plight. He spent nearly half a decade on the run. Eventually, in 1921, he was captured and remained in close confinement until his death in the autumn of 1936. Tragically, this was also the same year that Ethiopia was about to enter into its winter of discontent. But before that happened a new emperor had to be chosen.

After the overthrow of Lij Iyasu, Menelik's daughter, Zawditu, became empress, and Tafari Makonnen, the son of Menelik's cousin Ras Makonnen, became regent and heir to the throne and was given the title of Ras or (Prince) Tafari. It was a

The Palace of Emperor Menelik II, Addis Ababa, c. 1900 *Menelik II chose Addis Ababa ("New Flower") as his capital. In its first years it was more like a military encampment than a town. After Menelik's victory over Italy at the Battle of Adwa in 1896, European delegations and businessmen hurried to Addis Ababa seeking all types of concessions and contracts to modernize the nation. The French delegation was the first to arrive, bringing a handsome Sèvres china service as a gift. The British mission followed with polar-bear skins and gold-inlaid rifles. The head of the mission recorded that the emperor "was particularly pleased with four silver-gilt rice bowls; so much more useful, he pointed out, than the musical boxes and mechanical toys which were the usual stock-in trade of foreign visitors."*

These photographs of the palace were taken by Major C.W. Gwynn. The Royal Geographical Society honored Gwynn in 1907 for his survey work "carried out under very difficult conditions in the region of the Blue Nile and the Sudan-Abyssinian frontier."

Audience Chamber, The Palace, Addis Ababa, c. 1900   *In 1898 Great Britain appointed its first ambassador to Ethiopia. It took him sixteen days to travel the 260 miles to reach the inland capital from the Red Sea. A member of the mission wrote the following:*

The first appearances of the representative of the British Empire in Addis Ababa was not impressive. We . . . arrived like a flock of half-drowned hens wading through a sea of mud as a continuous sheet of water (a sample of what are flippantly called the 'light rains') [transformed] an extraordinarily rich and thirsty soil. We were obliged to beg for a couple of days' grace for the prosaic business of drying clothes and luggage, and furnishing the large round empty hut assigned to us, an operation performed by dividing up the space and extemporizing packing-cases into divans and cupboards. The third day the king sent word that he would receive the envoy at his palace. The reception took place about nine o'clock, but at early dawn our compound was surrounded by a variegated mob of men armed with samples of all the guns, ancient and modern, dressed in flowing shammas ornamented by a broad stripe. Among them appeared officers with with brocaded shields overlaid with gold and silver on their arms, and mounted on fat mules gorgeous with brass and silver trappings. Interspersed were the men of distinguished service—lion-killers with position and title he would hold for the next thirteen years until he was crowned Emperor Haile Selassie I.

Though Empress Zawditu held sovereign power, Ras Tafari was doubtless the more able leader. Younger than the empress by almost twenty years, he soon emerged as the more active political figure. In particular, he was in charge of foreign affairs. When foreign visitors arrived in Ethiopia, the regent graciously received them, and in return they tended to give him their support and admiration. They welcomed him as the first ruler of his country, at least since the Aksumite Kingdom, to speak a European Language—in this case, French. When Tafari was a young boy his father arranged for a French tutor by the name of Dr. Vitalien, a citizen of Guadeloupe, to be brought into the house to teach French. Abba Samuel, an Ethiopian teacher attached to the French Mission, supplemented the work of Dr. Vitalien. Therefore, by the time Ras Tafari became regent he was well versed in both European modernization via the French language and Western education, as well as the traditional values associated with being a descendent of Ethiopian royal family. Ras Tafari, especially after he became Emperor Haile Selassie I, was to walk this tightrope between these two worldviews for the rest of his life, always conscious of how they complemented and conflicted with each other. Mostly, he used this sense of *"double-consciousness"* to his own advantage. In particular, he was able to continue the work of modernization begun by Menelik without giving the sense of abandoning the

---

a fringe of the animal's mane round their heads like a blonde wig of a bald-headed comedian; elephant-killers with chains hanging from their ears; and warriors with feathers and bangles awarded for various feats of prowess. . . .

The reception took place in a large whitewashed hall, situated on a commanding hill, and fenced by a high splitbamboo Zeriba, whitewashed walls, floors strewed with rugs, and the roof of gaily coloured matted bamboo supported by wooden pillars. The officers and ministers, in full panoply of state, grouped themselves according to rank. The lines converging toward an alcove, under which, huddled between two high cushions on a throne, like a richly hung four-post bed, sat the king. His majesty, though very dark in complexion with not very regular features, has charming manners and a particularly pleasant voice . . . a most intelligent mobile expression and an amicable smile that makes his features almost handsome. The audience was very short. The credentials were delivered and accepted with friendly expressions of the usual sort, the (Italian) cannon boomed a salute, and the ceremony that opened a new chapter in the history of the respective nations was over.

traditional values of his country and alienating the people of Ethiopia the way Lij Iyasu had.

One of his first steps was to recruit Russian officers to train his troops. In the years following he established an Imperial Bodyguard, a modern force composed largely of Ethiopians who had served with the British in Kenya or the Italians in Libya. Tafari's most spectacular achievement came on September 28, 1923. He succeeded in gaining Ethiopia's entry into the League of Nations, which had been founded only four years earlier. Becoming part of the League of Nations proved that Tafari had foresight in regard to foreign affairs. In later years, this international organization would provide him with a valuable platform in his efforts to defend his country against the encroaching tide of fascism that threatened Ethiopia just prior to World War II.

Tafari emerged as a modernizer in other fields as well. He founded a modern printing press, the *Berhanenna Salam*, or *"Light and Peace,"* in 1923. It printed an Amharic newspaper with the same title that carried articles popularizing the cause of reform. Also during Tafari's reign as regent, a steady flow of literary, religious, and educational books in Amharic were published.

Other institutions that were established during this time included a modern hospital, the *Bet Sayda*, founded in 1924, and a new secondary school, the Tafari Makonnen, in 1925. English and French were the languages used to teach students in the Tafari Makonnen. Also, during this period Ras Tafari took steps to abolish the age-old institution of slavery. He established a bureau and a school for freed slaves.

Ras Tafari steadily gained support for his future bid to become emperor of Ethiopia. Empress Tawditu recognized his enhanced position, and on October 6, 1928, she bestowed upon him the title of *Negus,* or "king." The following year he established an Ethiopian air force. This helped him further consolidate his power and became a deciding factor in the Battle of Anchim in March 1930. In that engagement Zawditu's ex-husband, Ras Gugsa Wale, a challenger to the throne, was defeated and killed. A few days later, Empress Zawditu died.

In the midst of all this death and defeat Negus Tafari ascended the imperial throne as Emperor Haile Selassie. On November 2, 1930, the emperor's coronation was held in the capital city of Addis Ababa. The Duke of Gloucester for Britain, the Prince of Udine for Italy, and Marshal Franchet d'Esperey for France attended the ceremony. Representatives also came from Sweden, Holland, Belgium, Germany, Poland, Greece, Turkey, Egypt, the United States, Russia, and Japan. The celebrations attracted international media coverage for both the emperor and his country. Strange to think that the countries, with the possible exception of Sweden, who sent representatives to the coronation would, in less than a decade, be engaged in the greatest cataclysmic event in world history. For the people of Ethiopia it would be less than six years before terror struck their country again.

But for the moment, Ethiopia basked in the worldwide attention given to the coronation, especially Ras Tafari's adoption of the imperial title of *Haile Selassie,* or *"Power of the Trinity."* Ethiopia became far better known than it ever had been before, particularly in Africa, where many regarded the country as an island of independence in a sea of European colonialism. Even as far away as Jamaica, where Marcus Garvey's *"Back to Africa Movement"* was by then well established, many saw the coronation as no less than a realization of the biblical prophecy that *"kings would come out of Africa."* An interesting consequence of this was the founding of the Rastafarian Movement, a social movement that combines various elements of religious prophecy, specifically the idea of a black God and Messiah. Rastafarians believe in the *Kebra Nagast* as the sacred text of the African people, and they saw Haile Selassie's ascension to the throne of Ethiopia as a sign that the *"redemption of the African race was therefore at hand."*

Identifying themselves passionately with the new Ethiopian monarch, as well as with Ethiopia's status as an independent African State, they rejected traditional European Christianity and celebrated instead a religion with the spirituality and redemption of African people as its central focus. In the Rastafarian sacred text, it is the people of Africa and of the African Diaspora who are the chosen of God. This movement later gained considerable strength, especially after Bob Marley, one of its most avid proponents, helped to spread the message around the world through his music.

In the meantime, during the year following the coronation, Emperor Haile Selassie introduced the country's first written constitution:

> In this constitution which we are giving to the Ethiopian people, the principal ideas formulated in it are the following:
>
> (1) It is to bring about that, Ethiopia being one family undivided by sections, the people shall live in unity controlled by one law and governed by one Emperor, and that this power of unity shall be safeguarded by the interests which bind them permanently together, and while the interest of the individual shall not be abandoned, the strength of the United community shall be paramount. Without sacrificing the benefits due to individuals or oneself, one is not to seek divisive private interests.

This was the first article of the Ethiopian Constitution. It stated in words what Menelik and the first two great kings of Ethiopia, Tewodros and Yohannes IV, had been able only to dream about, a unified Ethiopia. It was a living symbol that those dreams would finally come true. Menelik's memory must have lingered a long time over the drafting and signing of the country's first written constitution. It was his struggle to create a unified modern state, and his unyielding faith in the Ethiopian people, that laid the foundation for this momentous occasion. The fact that a statue of him was unveiled during the coronation ceremonies attests to the deep reverence in which he was held. Though he did not live long enough to see his dream reach fruition, the constitution and his monument outside the ministry of education were a strong indication that he would remain a part of his country's history, a history he helped make.

The constitution was enacted on July 16, 1931. In it Emperor Haile Selassie was officially described as a descendent of King Solomon and the queen of Sheba, and—almost in an effort to clarify this point—Article 7 of the constitution states,

> This constitution which we have established is not just idle fiction or discordant with the country's customs, for it closely approaches that of the civilized and educated nations, in its preparation we had the help and ideas of our nobles and our officials and of other Ethiopian subjects whom we had chosen for their relevant knowledge. Man makes a beginning, but it is God alone who has the power to accomplish things, we place our trust in God that he may grant us to bring into effect this constitution which we have set up.

Ethiopian Musicians, c. 1900 *This group of musicians was photographed by L. Naretti in his Massawa studio. The instrument in the center is a stringed* beganna. *This lyre is considered to be a God-given instrument that descended to the Ethiopians from biblical King David It is a plucked instrument normally used to accompany singing.*

6

THE SONS OF
SHEBA'S RACE

But in the wake of your sacrifice
May all Africa arise
With blazing eyes and night-dark face
In answer to the call of Sheba's race
Langston Hughes (1902–1967)

After Haile Selassie's coronation and the signing of the country's first written constitution, Ethiopia seemed destined for a long period of peace and prosperity, especially after all the worldwide attention it had received. But, unfortunately, this was not going to happen, because once again the will of the people of Ethiopia was about to be tested. This approaching crisis had been set in motion at least five years before the new emperor ascended the throne, and it involved the British and Italian governments. Reverting to a policy dating back to the nineteenth century, they persuaded the League of Nations to ban the export of firearms to several African states, including Ethiopia. With no access to weapons to use in defense of recently celebrated independence, the people of Ethiopia would be placed in a vulnerable position. But the restriction on Ethiopian arms imports was rigidly enforced by the two colonial powers—not a difficult task, since between the two of them they controlled most of the territory on Ethiopia's borders.

Of course, Ras Tafari opposed this maneuver. In an address to the League of Nations, he explained that such restrictions were incompatible with his country's membership in the league. In this argument Ethiopia did not stand alone—the French Government again came to the aid of its old ally. It has been suggested that France did so partly because the arms trade was profitable and partly because it was considered a means of maintaining Ethiopia's friendship. Whatever its reasons, the country's opposition to the arms embargo proved decisive. The League of Nations agreed to exclude Ethiopia from the restricted zone.

But less than a year later another crisis erupted between Ethiopia and the two colonial powers. This time it was over territory. The British supported Italy's demand to construct a railway to link the Italian colonies of Eritrea and Somalia, west of Addis Ababa. In return, the Italian Government agreed to support Great Britian's plan to build a dam on Lake Tana. Tafari immediately protested to the League of Nations. He pointed out, once again with support of France, that the British and Italian agreement, entered into without consulting Ethiopia, a fellow member of the league, was in violation of the principles of that international body. He inquired whether members of the league desired "means of coercion" to be applied against Ethiopia "which they would undoubtedly dislike if applied against themselves."

His argument was persuasive. The British and Italian governments, embarrassed by his strongly worded reaction, protested their innocence of trying to exert pressure on Ethiopia and, at least on the surface, abandoned their plans. Even though these conflicts were resolved in Ethiopia's favor, they still compromised the nation's sense of peace and prosperity. More importantly, these two minor skirmishes were just the first rumblings of an impending storm, signs of which could already be seen gathering on the horizon of Africa's oldest independent Christian country. Whether the people of Ethiopia were ready to

Clock Tower and Palace, Addis Ababa, c. 1900 *In 1902 the British secured what they wanted from Emperor Menelik II—control of Lake Tana in northwestern Ethiopia. Control of the lake, a major source of the Blue Nile, meant cotton—and prosperity—for Egypt and the Sudan. The silt and mud deposits carried down by the Blue Nile from the Ethiopian Highlands fertilized the green belt that curls along the Nile's course. The Treaty of 1902 secured this flow of the Blue Nile for England. France and Italy recognized Great Britain's rights to the principal source of the Blue Nile in the Tripartite Treaty of 1906.*

acknowledge it or not, these storm warnings foreshadowed an inevitable clash between Ethiopia and the two colonial powers that were slowly but steadily encroaching on the country's hard-won independence.

Ethiopia had fought for and obtained its independence in the Battle of Adwa in 1896. Since that time the people of Ethiopia had worked hard to preserve their national heritage and consolidate the freedoms they had won. The unveiling of a monument of Menelik II, Ethiopia's first national hero, and the creation of the country's first written constitution, which proclaimed all Ethiopians equal under the law, symbolized their efforts.

Moreover, not only had the people of Ethiopia worked to create a sense of peace and prosperity within the borders of their own country, but also through the leadership of Emperor Haile Selassie, they had reached out in the spirit of friendship and cooperation to other countries and other nations.

As a result, Ethiopia gradually emerged as a symbol, an island of freedom and independence in a raging sea of colonialism. This symbol held special significance for other African countries whose people had fallen prey to the sword and gun of foreign invaders. It also shone with a special radiance for the people of Jamaica as they waged their own struggle for independence.

By any definition Ethiopia had reached a pinnacle in its struggle to become part of the modern world. Even for a people with such a long and varied history this new vision of itself as defender of freedom and independence must have seemed like a miraculous event, especially considering the obstacles they had to overcome. Yet, in spite of these accomplishments, the country was never more than one night's sleep away from a yawning abyss that threatened to swallow it whole, freedom, independence, and all—war with Italy.

A confrontation with this dreaded event seemed inevitable. The country was dangerously situated between two Italian colonies, Eritrea to the north and Somalia to the southeast. Part of the conflict between the Ethiopian and Italian governments was that neither one of these territories could be developed in isolation from Ethiopia, nor expanded other than at Ethiopia's expense.

Italy, a latecomer to the scramble for colonies in Africa, was desperate to keep up with the other colonial powers. As a result, the Italians established their first colony at Eritrea in the 1890s, and planned to use Eritrea as a base for further expansion. But the Battle of Adwa had proved a turning point in the history of Ethiopian and Italian relations. Prior to the battle, Italy had sought to gain control of Ethiopia first through Article 17 of the Wichale Treaty and later through military action. After both of these failed, Italy turned just as ambitiously to economic penetration. By this time it had gained the support of Great Britain. The British sided with the Italians in exchange for Italy's support for a proposed British dam at Lake Tana. Caught between the ambitions of these two colonial powers, Ethiopia was caught in an ever tightening noose. It was only a matter of time before the trapdoor would fall. All that was missing was the right incentive. Benito Mussolini and the rise of the *National Fascist Party (Partito Nazionale Fascista)* (PNF) provided the necessary catalyst.

The Italian dictator coined the term *fascism* in 1919. At that time, Italy had recently emerged from World War I physically and economically exhausted. Mussolini developed the political ideology of fascism as means to help revive the social, economic, and cultural life of his country. Italians looked to the *old Roman Empire* as a model of what they wanted their new Italy to be like. In fact, the word *fascism* refers to the ancient Roman symbol of power, the *fasces*, a bundle of sticks bound to an ax, which represented civic unity and the authority of Roman officials to punish wrongdoers. The term also comes from the Italian word *fascio*, which means "union" or "league."

After the government of Benito Mussolini assumed power in Italy, the spirit of the colonial government in Eritrea changed. The new administration stressed the racial and political superiority of the Italian people. Segregation became the hard-and-fast rule, and the people of Eritrea were regulated to the lowest rungs of society in their own homeland. This was only a preliminary stage. Driven by the desire to restore their empire to its former greatness, it was only a matter of time before the people of Italy received the call to *"revenge Adwa,"* and embarked on a new war of conquest. From the outset Mussolini seemed determined to make good on his intention to create an African empire worthy of the descendents of ancient Rome.

That intention was influenced by the situation in Europe. The climate of international affairs during the first years of the

The Italian Infirmary, Massawa, c. 1900   *Italy's first modern colonial venture was the takeover of the Red Sea port of Massawa in 1885. Southern Italian politicians favored colonial expansion as an outlet for the population explosion in their region, and Northern Italian politicians wanted Italy to become a great world power that would include an overseas empire. Massawa remained under Italian rule from 1885 to 1941, when the city passed to British rule. In 1952 it was incorporated into the federation of Ethiopia and Eritrea. The port exports agricultural products, especially nuts, hides, and coffee.*

1930s provided Italy with assurance that aggression against Ethiopia could be undertaken without much risk of censor from the other colonial powers, not even France. This was primarily the case because Adolf Hitler became chancellor of Germany in January 1933, which meant that Mussolini had the support of a powerful ally. And equally important was the fact that the French and British governments became increasingly reluctant to take any stand against Mussolini for fear of driving him into an allegiance with the Germans—with whom he was already linked anyway by a common fascist doctrine.

This was a dreadful and unexpected about-face as far as Ethiopia was concerned, because up to that point France had supported Ethiopian independence and had been its staunchest ally against pressures from Italy, and to a lesser extent Great Britain. Now the people watched as the French Government, becoming increasingly concerned with the situation in Europe, changed its policy. To please Mussolini, France began to with-draw opposition to Italian expansion in Ethiopia, and proposed that Italy in return should waive its interest in the French Colony of Tunisia. As a result, Ethiopia stood in the breach alone.

On October 3, 1935, the Fascist army began its long ex-pected invasion, without a formal declaration of war. The main frontal attack was launched from Eritrea and was at first directed by Marshal Emilio De Bono. Initially, as a result of Ethiopian resistance, the Italian advance ground almost to a halt. De Bono had seized Aksum, forty miles within Ethiopia, on October 15, 1935, but it took him over three weeks, until November 8, to capture Maquale, a little more than thirty-seven miles farther south. Mussolini, frustrated by this painfully slow progress, dismissed De Bono and replaced him with an Italian general by the name of Pietro Badoglio.

In the meantime, Emperor Haile Selassie worked desperately to organize Ethiopian resistance in the face of overwhelming odds. Armed mostly with rifles, the Ethiopian army was no match for the airplanes, bombs, flame-throwers, and poison gas of the Italians. Town after town fell to the enemy, and thousands of Ethiopians died defending their country against the invaders.

The Ethiopian army, though faced by a more powerful enemy in full command of the air, succeeded at the end of 1935 in launching a major counteroffensive aimed at isolating the Italian position at Maquale. The Ethiopian Christmas Offensive, as it is sometimes called, drove the enemy back from the Takkaze River. The invaders, however, rallied all of their forces, and with the use of their artillery, tanks, bombing, and mustard gas, halted the Ethiopian advance. On January 24, 1936, the people of Ethiopia had been decisively defeated.

Less than five short years after the coronation of Emperor Haile Selassie, the unveiling of the monument of Emperor Menelik, and the creation of the country's first written constitution, Ethiopia's fate rested in the hands of its enemies. Thousands of Ethiopians—men, women, and children, soldiers and civilians—had died in the process.

On May 2, 1936, Emperor Haile Selassie, who had returned to Addis Ababa in April, left the capital city to escape the invaders. He also left to plead the cause of Ethiopia before the world. His family and several of his closest associates accompanied him. Three days after the emperor's departure, Italian tanks rolled down the paved streets of Addis Ababa. Four days later Mussolini proclaimed the successful end of the war and triumphantly declared, "Ethiopia is Italian." From that point forward, any Ethiopians continuing to resist were treated as rebels and were liable for immediate execution.

On June 30, 1936, Emperor Haile Selassie made an impassioned speech before the League of Nations in Geneva, Switzerland. His speech read in part,

> I, Haile Selassie I, Emperor of Ethiopia, am here today to claim that justice which is due to my people, and the assistance promised it eight months ago, when fifty nations asserted that aggression had been committed in violation of international affairs.

After a brief pause he continued to outline, in considerable detail, the crimes that had been committed against the Ethiopian people.

It was at the time when the operations for the encircling of Maquale were taking place that the Italian command, fearing a riot, followed the procedure which it is now my duty to denounce to the world. Special sprayers were installed on board aircraft so that they could vaporize, over vast areas of territory, a fine, death-dealing rain. Groups of nine, fifteen, eighteen aircraft followed one another so that the fog issuing from them formed a continuous sheet. It was thus that, as from the end of January, 1936, soldiers, women, children, cattle, rivers, lakes and pastures were drenched continually with this deadly rain. In order to kill off systematically all living creatures, in order to more surely to poison waters and pastures, the Italian command made its aircraft pass over and over again. That was its chief method of warfare.

From the outset, Italy's unprovoked attack, the League of Nations' lack of intervention, and the Fascist use of poison gas made a deep impact on the world's opinion toward the war. Societies dedicated to the support of Ethiopia were founded in Britain, the United States, Holland, and a number of other countries.

The invasion also had a significant impact on the people of Africa and among people of African descent throughout the world. For the longest time Ethiopia had been for them a symbol of freedom and independence. Now that image was seriously threatened with extinction. It was not a defeat to be taken lightly. For example, in a study of Harlem life during the Depression era, the African-American journalist Roi Ottley indicated that the Italo-Ethiopian crisis aroused enormous indignation, stirring the emotions of African Americans like no other event of the time, not even the disturbing Scottsboro, Alabama, rape case in 1931. From the beginning of the controversy, wrote Ottley, the fate of the world's last independent black stronghold was of burning concern to New York's burgeoning African-American community. By the time of the Italian invasion in October 1935, Ethiopia's survival had become a topic of angry debate in poolrooms, barbershops, taverns, and on street corners as well as in the boardrooms and salons of the

Ethiopian Musicians, c. 1899   *These musicians were photographed in southern Ethiopia. They are playing a small beganna.*

№ 183. Donne abissine portatrici di miese ed anghera
(Fot. S. Naretti. Massaua)

Women Porters, c. 1899 *These Ethiopian women are carrying grain and water. Naretti's photographs captured the people and their customs. They help us to visualize a unique period of history of more than a hundred years ago. In the 1890s Massawa became a tourist spa for wealthy northern Italians seeking a warmer winter climate. Perhaps Naretti sold his photographs, which were printed on a heavy paper, as souvenirs.*

local elite. One of America's greatest poets, who made his home in Harlem, was inspired to write a poem about Ethiopia that included the following lines:

> But in the wake of your Sacrifice
> May all Africa arise
> With blazing eyes and night-dark face
> In answer to the call of Sheba's race.

Street Scene, Harar, c. 1905   *Harar, in eastern Ethiopia, is the nation's only walled city. The ancient walls, with six gates, enclose a crowded Muslim town with alleyways that wind to a central marketplace.*

Sir Richard Burton (1821–1890), the famed English scholar and explorer, published forty-three volumes about his explorations throughout Arabia, India, and Africa. In 1860 Burton traveled by stagecoach to Salt Lake City, Utah. His resulting volume, City of Saints *(1861) dealt with his observations of the Mormon Church and its leader, Brigham Young. In 1845 Burton became the first European to enter Harar without being executed. Harar had the reputation of being a Muslim citadel that forbade access to non-Muslims. Burton described his adventures in* First Footsteps in East Africa *(1856).*

7

LIBERATION

Just as a person who is always asserting that he is too good-natured is the very one from whom to expect, on some occasion, the coldest and most unconcerned cruelty, so when any group sees itself as the bearer of civilization this very belief will betray it into behaving barbarously at the first opportunity.

Simone Weil (1909–1943)

In spite of widespread opposition, most countries around the world recognized Italy's *"conquest"* of Ethiopia. Most notable among these was Great Britain, who stated its acceptance of Italy's control of Ethiopia in 1938. A few countries, however, refused to recognize Italy's right to rule Ethiopia. They were the United States, the Soviet Union, Mexico, New Zealand, and Haiti.

Regardless of the world's reaction, Italian occupation of Ethiopia led to fundamental political, social, economic, and religious changes. Italian-occupied Ethiopia was officially merged with Eritrea and Somalia into an entirely new territory called *Africa Orientale Italiana (AOI)* or *Italian East Africa.* For the first time in history, this brought the greater part of the Horn of Africa under a single administration. This area was then divided into six separate provinces: (1) Eritrea, including the former Ethiopian province of Tegray, with its capital at Asmara; (2) Amhara, formed out of the old provinces of Bagemder, Gojjam, Wallo, and northern Shawa, with its capital at Gondar; (3) Galla and Sidamo, with a capital at Jemma; (4) Addis Ababa, later named Shawa; (5) Harar; and (6) Somalia, including Ogaden, with a capital at Mogadishu. As a result of these arrangements, Ethiopia, as far as the Italians were concerned, ceased to be a legal entity.

Suddenly and irrevocably, the people of Ethiopia found themselves in a terrible quagmire in which their long, illustrious history and national heritage were being deliberately dismantled right before their very eyes. In fact, from the very beginning, Mussolini made every effort to remove or destroy all symbols of Ethiopia's historic independence. He gave personal orders to remove two of Addis Ababa's most important monuments. The first one was of Emperor Menelik II, the Ethiopian hero who had defeated the Italians at the Battle of Adwa. The second was a statue of the Lion of Judah, which was significant because *"The Conquering Lion of Judah"* and *"King of Kings"* were among the titles Emperor Haile Selassie adopted at the time of his coronation. The statue also symbolized the relationship between Ethiopia and biblical prophecy that was written about in the *Kebra Nagast*, that kings and princes would come out of Egypt, and Ethiopia would stretch out her hands to God.

Based on the *"ravage and terror"* that the Italians carried out during this time, it seemed that they were motivated by the assumption that if you destroy the symbol then you destroy the message. Mussolini later gave orders for the looting, and shipping to Rome, of one of the great obelisks of Aksum. The other *"loot"* taken to Rome included the already mentioned Lion of Judah monument, five Ethiopian royal crowns, and a number of paintings that had adorned the walls of the Ethiopian Parliament.

In spite of the Italians' aggressive tactics, Ethiopian resistance continued throughout the occupation. On May 4, 1936, a group of Ethiopians led by Lej Hayla Maryman Mammo attacked members of the invading army on their way to Addis Ababa, the capital city. Although the attack was unsuccessful, it

earned Mammo the title of the *first aragna,* or *patriot of Shawa.*
From that point forward, until they defeated the Italians, the
resistance fighters were known as patriots.

In an effort to crush Ethiopian opposition, Rodolfo Graziani,
who had been appointed Italian viceroy, issued a proclamation
that Italy was the "absolute master of Ethiopia" and would
"remain so at whatever cost." If necessary, he would use
"extreme severity towards anyone who resisted, but the greatest
generosity" to Ethiopians who submitted to Italian authority.
Mussolini agreed with this policy and telegraphed his approval
while emphasizing that "all rebel prisoners must be shot."

Undeterred by threats of violence, Ethiopian patriots continued their struggle against Italian occupation. During the rainy
season of 1936 an attempt was made to recapture Addis Ababa.
On July 28 patriots launched an attack from the northwest but
were repulsed by machine-gun fire. Almost a month later one
of Emperor Menelik's former commanders, Dajazmach Balcha,
launched another unsuccessful assault. Although both of these
attacks failed to achieve their objective, they were enough to
inspire the Ethiopians to keep fighting.

On February 19, 1937, two Eritreans, Abraha Daboch and
Moges Asgadom, attempted to assassinate Rodolfo Graziani;
this opened a new phase in the struggle. Reacting violently to
the attempted assassination of their leader, the Italians carried
out a three-day massacre. When it was over more than thirty
thousand Ethiopians had been murdered. Many survivors fled
the capital and joined ranks with the patriots. Strengthened by
this increase in their numbers, the patriots again took the offensive during the rainy season of 1937. As a result, Mussolini
ordered Graziani to use all measures at his disposal, including
poison gas. Even though the viceroy intensified his reign of
ravage and terror, the war had turned against the Italians.
Graziani was unable to crush the rebellion. Instead, he entered
into negotiations with the area's principal leader, Ras Ababa
Aragay. During much of this phase of the struggle, Emperor
Haile Selassie remained in exile in Great Britain. The emperor
continued to gain support of the western powers, but substan-
tial support failed to materialize, partly because at this point

Europe was embroiled in its own concerns. Hitler had already made massive preparations for war. It was just a matter of time before he pulled the trigger and set into motion the second cataclysmic event of the century. Consequently, the emperor's demands for support for his people fell on deaf ears. Thoughts of a second world war loomed large in the hearts and minds of the people of Europe and the rest of the world. Thoughts of war also loomed large in the hearts and minds of the patriots fighting for freedom in Ethiopia. They understood that the coming war would have a profound impact on their struggle against the Italian invaders.

In the meantime, however, the occupying forces took the offensive once again after the summer rains. But the patriots did not lose hope. Well informed about the growing conflict in Europe, they were confident that ultimately they would receive the assistance they so desperately needed.

The patriots had established their base of operations primarily in Shawa, Gojjam, and Bagemder. But during this phase of the struggle, they attracted support from almost every part of Ethiopia. Some of the most committed fighters included Eritrean deserters from the colonial army. There was also an active underground movement situated in the capital city and a few other areas. This movement was primarily composed of what the Ethiopian's referred to as *wust arbagna,* or *"insider patriots."* Their function was to provide military, medical, and other assistance to the fighters in the field and to keep them informed of the enemy's movements. Many Ethiopian women were prominent, both in the field, where they fought side by side with their brothers, uncles, fathers, and sons, and as *wust patriots,* living lives of constant danger. But the people of Ethiopia—men, women, and children—were unrelenting in their struggle for liberation.

It was primarily because of their unyielding resistance that the duke of Aosta replaced Graziani as viceory on the day after Christmas in 1937. By then the patriots controlled most of Shawa and Amhara, and there were large pockets of resistance in other parts of the country as well. So extensive was the support for the Ethiopian patriots that Menelik's great-grandson, Lej Yohannes Iyasu, himself a patriot, observed that the Italians, though in control of several major towns, had never been able to control the country or conquer the Ethiopian people. This continued resistance on the part of the people of Ethiopia drove a wedge between the Italians and their dreams of empire. With each passing day, the gulf that separated them grew wider and wider. Rumors of the approaching war did nothing to relieve the sense of doom and defeat they felt. Their increasing sense of desperation hung over all of their efforts like a malignant shadow. Long before the last shot, they knew that the great *"Roman"* army had tasted the meat of bitter defeat.

Nevertheless, in spite of their extensive support, the patriots understood that the battle was far from over. In fact, by 1939, the year Hitler invaded Poland and initiated the start of World War II, the struggle against the Italian invaders had reached a stalemate. The Italians had failed to defeat the patriots, but at the same time, the patriots were unable to expel the invaders out of their country. Even so, the advantage had definitely shifted in favor of the patriots. Though the Italians continued to maintain a presence inside Ethiopia, that presence had been reduced to life inside a series of well-guarded ports. Some reports suggest that an estimated sixty-five Italian battalions were compelled to live inside forts. The situation was so serious that the duke of Aosta advised Mussolini against entering into the war because subduing the rebels would demand too much of the army's attention.

In the early morning hours of September 1, 1939, the German armies marched into Poland. On September 3, 1939, the British and French governments surprised Hitler by declaring war on Germany. Even though a close ally of Nazi Germany, Mussolini was still too preoccupied with his own concerns to involve Italy in the war. However, he managed to announce to the world that his country was in a state of *"pre-belligerency,"* by which he meant that he was committed to entering the war at some future date. By postponing Italy's involvement, Mussolini delayed any potential conflict with France and avoided any immediate allied attack on

Ethiopian Soldiers, c. 1910 *This photograph of an Ethiopian chief and his soldiers was taken near the Kenya-Ethiopian border, c. 1910. Between 1896 and 1910, Ethiopia expanded to its present size, absorbing the Highlands, key river systems, and a buffer of low-lying arid zones around the nation's central core. N. C. Cockburn, the photographer, was a member of several British East African surveying groups (1909–1910) who fixed the border between Kenya and Ethiopia.*

the vulnerable Italian East African empire, where the Ethiopian patriots were still unyielding in their struggle for independence. He maintained this course of action until Germany defeated France in the summer of 1940. With Hitler's victory, Mussolini anticipated a quick end to the war, and he declared war on Britain and France on June 10, 1940.

Mussolini's declaration of war was an event the Ethiopian patriots had been awaiting. It would prove to be not only a turning point in their struggle against the Italian Fascist but, more profoundly, a turning point in Ethiopian history. The British

Communal Hut, 1899 *This Ethiopian communal hut was photographed by Major R.G.T. Bright in the southern part of the country near the Kenya border. For these thatched huts, the women weave strips of colored cloth into a mat. The patterned side is placed over the wooden frame so as to be visible within the hut while the rough fibers are exposed like thatch on the outside.*

Government, following Mussolini's lead, abandoned its long-standing attitude toward Italian involvement in Ethiopia. For more than twenty-five years Britain had supported Italian expansion in Ethiopia. The opening hostilities in the summer of 1940 forced the British to reconsider their relationship with Ethiopia. This shift in attitude was inspired primarily by British self-interest. The Italians in East Africa threatened Britain's important sea route to India and were in a position to overrun

Ethiopian Houses, Gore, 1899 *Gore is a town in the west-central part of Ethiopia near the border with the Sudan. Major R.G.T. Bright took this photograph while surveying what would become the permanent boundary between the Sudan and Ethiopia.*

British territories in Kenya, British Somaliland, and the Sudan. So a change in attitude seemed prudent at the time and mutually beneficial for both countries.

Their first response was to offer assistance to the Ethiopian patriots. If nothing else, this offer of assistance boosted the morale of the patriots. Throughout their previous four-year struggle, they had taken every opportunity to isolate, besiege, and eventually demoralize the Italian invaders. They had been able to accomplish this remarkable feat while fighting against overwhelming odds. Compared to the Italian Army and the Italian Royal Air force, the Ethiopian patriots were ill-equipped and ill-trained. When they finally received British military assistance, they were able to take the offensive.

Ethiopian and British cooperation produced the desired result in the second half of January 1941. The British and Ethiopian forces launched three major, almost simultaneous attacks against Italian East Africa occupied territory. As a result, the advance to the Ethiopian capital city of Addis Ababa, which took the Italian forces seven months, took British and Ethiopian forces less than three months.

The Italians, defeated and demoralized, surrendered on April 4, 1941. Their surrender brought an end to Italian occupation of Ethiopia. Mussolini's once victorious army was reduced to a number of isolated and beleaguered garrisons.

On May 5, 1941, exactly five years to the day after the Italians had captured the capital city, Emperor Haile Selassie and the patriots of Ethiopia triumphantly returned to Addis Ababa.

Ethiopian Official with his Secretary, 1899   *This photograph was taken by Major R.G.T. Bright, who was honored by the Royal Geographical Society in 1906 for his more than six years of surveying work with several East African boundary commissions.*

8

THE AFTERMATH

The best way of learning to be an independent sovereign state is to be an independent sovereign state.

Kwame Nkrumah (1900–1972)

In the aftermath of the Fascist occupation of Ethiopia, Emperor Haile Selassie addressed an audience of Ethiopians with the following words:

Our people of Ethiopia! Listen!
Thanks be to Almighty God who is impartial to All.
Who can break the arms of the strong
And who stands by the oppressed.

After pausing for a few brief seconds to allow his audience to absorb the meaning of his words, the emperor continued.

When Our long-time enemy, Italy, crossed our border and occupied Our country by aggressive force, we fought to defend Our country as much as we could and then went to Europe to solicit help while you, patriots of Ethiopia, continued the struggle and waited for us fighting day and night in the forests and mountains against the military superior brutal enemy, in taking advantage of your natural heroism as your greatest weapon, never putting aside your swords, abandoning your flag or surrendering to alien rule. As you now see, your five-year struggle has made it possible for you to witness the fruits of your efforts and sacrifices.

He concluded his speech with the following declaration:

Long live independent Ethiopia! Long live Great Britain!

At the time it only seemed natural that the emperor would link his country's independence with Great Britain in the same declaration. After all, even though it was late in coming, Britain had provided Ethiopia with much needed military and economic assistance. As a result, the people of Ethiopia owed the people of Britain a debt of gratitude. So in that respect the emperor was completely justified in extending this show of appreciation to the British government. The two countries were old friends and allies. But in the weeks and months that followed his triumphant speech, Emperor Haile Selassie would have cause to regret those words linking his country, even symbolically, to Great Britain—and to an even greater degree he would come to regret the great obligation that his people owed to the rulers of the British Empire.

In the aftermath of Ethiopia's struggle of liberation, the relationship between Ethiopia and Great Britain became increasingly strained. There were several reasons for this, but the primary reason was that the two countries differed in their opinions about the future direction of Ethiopia. The Ethiopians, especially the Ethiopian patriots who had spent the last five years fighting for their country's freedom, expected to assume full sovereignty without delay. Ethiopia was their country, and they had made grave sacrifices to make sure it remained that way. They had not surrendered to the Italians, and they didn't see any reason to bow down to the British. Now the words "Long live Great Britain!" sounded like a curse in their ears. They didn't understand why the British didn't just go home and let them run their own country.

The British, too, at least in theory, believed in Ethiopia's independence, but they saw it only as a long-distance goal. In the meantime, they saw Ethiopia as needing British guidance and support. The best thing that the people of Ethiopia could do to further their cause, Britian advised, was to follow the lead of their friends and allies. Above all else, the people of Ethiopia needed to be patient.

To many Ethiopians it seemed that they had exchanged the yoke of one oppressor for that of another. Though the British had entered their country as liberators, they had in fact now replaced the Italians as an occupying power. It became increasingly obvious that the British government was trying to establish a virtual *"Protectorate"* over Ethiopia.

The first clash over this question occurred as early as May 11, 1941, when Haile Selassie appointed his postwar cabinet. The British representative sternly informed him that such appointments could not be made until a peace treaty had been signed with Italy. This confrontation was resolved through a compromise. The British accepted the appointments but chose to regard the Ethiopian ministers as merely advisors to the British military administration of the country.

Tensions were further increased when the British decided to dismantle and take out of the country equipment that had been installed by the Italians. The equipment included weapons and military and civilian transportation. As a result, Ethiopia was thus visibly impoverished by its liberators, who soon came to be regarded as the looters of the country. Matters were only made worse by the presence of white South African soldiers, recruited by the British, who attempted to maintain a policy of segregation instituted by the former invaders.

Some British officials even went so far as to suggest the partition of the country. There were plans to unite parts of Tegray with the highlands of Eritrea in order to form a new state under British protection. In the southeast, the British government suggested incorporating the already British-occupied Somalia to create a Greater Somalia trusteeship. At this point, it must have seemed to many Ethiopians that the only thing that had changed in their circumstances was the uniform of their oppressors.

The British began to resemble the Italians still more. For Ethiopia, as a result of its "liberation" by British troops, was firmly under British economic as well as political control. The country used British East African currency, which was issued solely by Barclay's Bank, a British institution. If Ethiopians wanted to travel by air outside their country they did so exclusively on British Overseas Aviation Corporation (BOAC). Virtually all political power was likewise in the hands of the British military, which went so far as to censor the emperor's private correspondence.

The words "Long live independent Ethiopia! Long live Great Britain!" must have haunted Haile Selassie and the people of Ethiopia many times during these desperate days. So must have these words, quoted from the same speech:

> Our people of Ethiopia
> you know how grim life is to people
> robbed of their government, independence
> and their motherland. The time has come
> now when each and everyone
> of us should protect and serve
> our beloved country, Ethiopia
> with zeal and vigour.

The emperor's speech, "The Golden Declaration," was written and delivered by Haile Selassie to honor the men, women, and children, who had sacrificed their lives for the liberation of their country. Thirty thousand, fifty thousand, a hundred or two hundred thousand—nobody knew for sure the exact number of lives that had been lost. The only thing certain was that every family in Ethiopia had been visited by the "ravage and terror" and the plague of death during the occupation. Nobody had been spared suffering. When the emperor returned to Ethiopia, he had written the speech expressly to honor those who had made such desperate sacrifices. But his speech was also supposed to have been a great clarion call, a thunderous and triumphant rallying cry to inspire the living with hope for the future of their country. Now, in the strange turn of events since then, the emperor's speech sounded more and more like an epitaph for the living than for the dead.

It became increasingly obvious that something needed to be done. Not only was the emperor's continued relationship with the British making it impossible to rule his country effectively, it was also undermining his authority with the people of Ethiopia. The longer he allowed the British to hold the reigns, the more the people of Ethiopia would distrust his intentions and his abilities to govern.

The emperor finally took a stand. He decided to confront the British and force them to establish a treaty between Ethiopia and Great Britain. When they continued to put him off, the emperor broadcast their reluctance to sign a treaty across the airwaves of Addis Ababa radio. Eventually the British came around. After much bargaining, an *Anglo-Ethiopian Agreement and Military Convention* was signed on January 31, 1942. The treaty recognized Ethiopia as an independent state and established that the emperor was free to form his own government. At the same time, however, the agreement specified the emperor's obligation to appoint British advisors, a British Commissioner of Police, British police officers, inspectors, judges, and magistrates. No other foreign advisors could be appointed without consultation with the British.

Not satisfied with this agreement, the emperor and his ministers decided to take another bite of the treaty apple. On May 25, 1944, they demanded a new treaty. Though it took nearly two years, a new treaty was eventually signed. In this second Anglo-Ethiopian Treaty the British relinquished many of the rights they had demanded in the first. The treaty thus marked the full resumption of Ethiopian independence. In a symbolic gesture of his displeasure with Great Britain, the emperor did not sign this new agreement but relegated that task to his prime minister, MaKonnen EndalKachew. It is also significant to note that from this point forward, Haile Selassie rejected any further subsidy from his former ally.

There was just one hitch as far as Ethiopia was concerned. The British were allowed to remain in control of Ogaden, the

Somali-inhabited area adjacent to Italian Somalia. Called the *"Reserved Area,"* this territory occupied almost one third of the entire country. British motives for wanting to keep Ogaden became apparent in the spring of 1946, when they proposed that the territory be placed under British trusteeship. This "Greater Somalia" plan, was immediately rejected by the Ethiopian Government. The United States and the Soviet Union also raised strong opposition to the British plan. They both claimed that this was a scheme designed to expand the British Empire at the expense of both Italy and Ethiopia. It was significant that these two super powers voiced their opposition to British expansion in the Mediterranean and the Red Sea areas, because both were destined to play major roles in the future of East Africa. But in the meantime, Britain, faced with such fierce opposition, abandoned its claims on most of Ogaden in 1948, and six years later the entire region was at last returned to Ethiopia.

For the first time in nearly two decades—from the beginning of the Italian invasion in 1935 to the time the British relinquished all claims of authority—Ethiopia was fully in charge of its own destiny. A lot had happened in those two decades, and Ethiopia had suffered the brunt of one terrible onslaught after another. But the time had finally come for the people of Ethiopia to make some much needed repairs to the crumbling fabric of their country. For almost two decades international affairs had determined life in Ethiopia. Now it was time for the emperor and his people to pay attention to the inner workings of the country.

Emperor Haile Selassie continued to push reforms aimed at centralizing the government and modernizing Ethiopia. As a result, the 1940s and early 1950s constituted an important period of postwar reconstruction. Even though the emperor had to walk a virtual tightrope between modernization and traditionalism, this period witnessed a steady, though certainly not rapid, economic growth. It should be noted that these developments took place primarily in and around Addis Ababa, the capital city, and a few other towns. Later on, this uneven development led to charges of unfair treatment by some of

Ethiopia's ethnic groups who felt they were being pushed to the sidelines. As the 1960s and the era of the super powers approached, the charges would become very volatile and a source of endless frustration to Haile Selassie and the government of Ethiopia.

In the meantime Selassie continued to push through his reforms. A number of new hospitals were established. The most prestigious was the country's first modern teaching hospital, named after the emperor's daughter, Princess Tsahay, who had served as a nurse in London during World War II. A Russian Red Cross hospital was also set up and named after Dajazmach Balcha, a man who had fought at Adwa and later as a patriot against the Fascists.

Light industries—notably cotton, sugar, cement, leather, and printing—were established. Many hotels and restaurants, shops and trading were also established. All of this led to an unprecedented growth in paid employment, and thereby encouraged urbanization. These developments, coupled with the considerable increase in the number of school and college graduates, brought about a significant change in the country's social structure.

It should also be noted that many of these developments were increasingly dependent upon American economic, military, and other assistance. In fact, a new government bank, the *State Bank of Ethiopia,* was run at first by an American governor, George Blowers. The majority of Ethiopian students studying abroad, including members of the military, went to the United States, and Ethiopian soldiers fought under American command in the Korean War.

In the aftermath of the terrible events of the past couple of decades, the people of Ethiopia had not only survived but had actually emerged victorious. But the road to recovery was a long and winding one, and the hardest part of their journey was still ahead. The next few years would prove to be crucial.

Muslim Official, c. 1902 *Islam was introduced into Ethiopia during the seventh century. Today more than one quarter of the population is Muslim, particularly those living in the Eastern Lowlands. Traditionally, the status of Islam has been far from equal with that of Christianity. About one tenth of Ethiopians are animists, who worship a variety of African deities. They live primarily in the Western Lowlands near the Sudanese border.*

Judaism has long been practiced in the vicinity of the ancient city of Gonder. Most of the Ethiopian Jews, known as Falasha, *emigrated to Israel between 1980 and 1992. Also known as* Beta Israel, *these people claim descent from Menelik I, traditionally considered the son of the queen of Sheba and King Solomon.*

9

Talking about a Revolution

If there is any period one would desire to be born in, is it not the age of Revolution, when the old and the new stand side by side, and admit of being compared, when the energies of all men are searched by fear and by hope, when the historic glories of the old can be compensated by the rich possibilities of the new era?

Ralph Waldo Emerson (1803–1882)

It is almost never when a state of things is the most detestable that it is smashed, but when, beginning to improve, it permits men to breathe, to reflect, to communicate their thoughts with each other and to gauge by what they already have the extent of their rights and their grievances. The weight, although less heavy, seems then all the more unbearable.

Alexis de Tocqueville (1805–1859)

The tide which is sweeping Africa today cannot be stayed. No power on earth is great enough to halt or to reverse the trend. Its march is as relentless and inexorable as the passage of time.

Emperor Haile Selassie: (To American Committee on Africa, 1960)

Ethiopia's journey from the ancient kingdom of Aksum to the twentieth century had been a long and arduous pilgrimage, punctuated by many traumas and triumphs along the way. From the early days of King Ezana's reign down through the ages of the Solomonic dynasties, the Ethiopian people fought to preserve their national heritage. They were confronted with numerous challenges. There were the relentless invasions from their Muslim neighbors. There was also the chaos from their own internal anarchy that threatened to destroy the very fabric of Ethiopian society. Along with these traumas Ethiopia also had its moments of glory. After all, this is the country that had been chosen to be the home of the Ark of the Covenant, a land of people who trace their lineage back to Menelik I, son of the queen of Sheba and King Solomon. For many, it is still the land of enchantment, the land of legend and myth, the land of Prester John. It has the great obelisks of the ancient kingdom of Aksum and the fabulous churches of Lalibala that some consider the eighth wonder of the world. Certainly, Ethiopia has much to cherish and glory in.

In the nineteenth century three great leaders were born in Ethiopia: Tewodros Yohannes IV, and Menelik II. Their collective contributions helped to unify the country in the time of its greatest turmoil known as the "Age of Princes." Menelik II also became renown for his defeat of the Italians at the Battle of Adwa. Because of his foresight and perseverance, Ethiopia marched with unbowed head into the modern era.

Although it was Menelik II who brought Ethiopia to the attention of the modern world, it was Haile Selassie I and the people of Ethiopia who picked up the gauntlet and continued the arduous journey into the twentieth century. After the restoration of Ethiopian independence, Haile Selassie I had to contend with several challenges to his authority, mostly due to the slow and uneven economic development taking place in the nation. Between 1941 and 1960 regional and ethnic conflicts reminiscent of the Age of Princes flared up. Even though

Selassie had attempted to create a sense of unity, many of Ethiopia's ethnic groups felt shortchanged, especially the nation's non-Amhara people, who felt they were excluded from the mainstream of Ethiopian life both economically and politically. Furthermore, many of the regional rulers felt threatened by the emperor's attempts to centralize the government by taking power from them and giving it to the lawmakers in Addis Ababa, who were loyal to the emperor. And many Ethiopians who lived in the developing urban areas felt that too many privileges were being granted to the nobility.

Students, especially students who had been educated in the United States and other parts of the world, complained about the slow progress of Ethiopia's social, political, and economic development. They pointed out that even though Ethiopia had maintained its independence longer than any other African nation, it still lagged behind these other countries when it came to economic development. They primarily blamed Haile Selassie and the government in Addis Ababa for the country's failure to keep up with modern times.

Whether they were right or wrong in this assessment, Ethiopian students were not the only ones to express it. Workers, taxi drivers, teachers, and soldiers began to voice similar dissatisfaction with the slow progress Ethiopia was making compared to other African countries. Many were angry that the Amhara, who made up only twenty percent of the population, dominated political life. Though there were over seventy languages in Ethiopia, Amharic was chosen as the country's official language. Some people also noticed that the Muslims, who now made up almost half of the population, were rarely if ever appointed to positions of power within the government. They also complained that Ethiopia had one of the lowest standards of living of any country in Africa.

Dealt with separately, these issues represented just the normal give and take of life in a diverse, multiethnic society. But taken together and coupled with the sheer intensity with which the people of Ethiopia expressed these issues, they represented

Oromo Man, c. 1900 *The Oromo (called pejoratively Galla) are one of the two largest linguistic groups of Ethiopia. They speak a language of the Cushitic branch of the Hamito-Semitic family. A Galea-English dictionary was compiled and published almost ninety years ago.*

By the seventeenth century, the Oromo occupied all of southern Ethiopia and most of the central and western provinces. Divisions among the Oromo facilitated their own eventual dominance by the people whom they had driven northward, the Amhara, the other major linguistic group in Ethiopia.

a virtual powder keg. And even Haile Selassie, with all of his mastery of diplomacy, could not forestall the explosion.

There were periodic signs of trouble. Regional leaders who resented the emperor for taking away their power led rebellions from time to time. As early as 1943, less than two years after Ethiopia won its liberation from Italy, there was an armed rebellion in Tegray Province known as the Weyane Revolt. It was crushed only with the help of the British Air Force. Parts of the Gojjam Province also rebelled, but the most serious revolt occurred in 1960. In December of that year, while Emperor Haile Selassie was in Brazil during a state visit, his Imperial Bodyguard staged a *coup* masterminded by Garmame Neway, an American-educated radical, whose brother Mengistu happened to be the head of the Imperial Guard.

The attempted takeover was supported by a large number of university students in Addis Ababa. The rebels seized the Imperial Palace, where they imprisoned twenty-one government officials, who for the most part had remained loyal to the emperor. The emperor's son, Crown Prince Asfa Wossen, was named by the leaders of the coup as the new head of the government. The prince read messages over the Addis Ababa airwaves in which he spoke of "corruption in government" and the "selfish people" who ran the country. However, it has been suggested that the rebels forced the prince to make these broadcasts.

After hearing of what had happened in his country, Emperor Haile Selassie returned to Ethiopia immediately. In the meantime, Ethiopia's army and air force, which for the most part had remained loyal to the emperor, crushed the rebellion on December 17, 1960. Before surrendering, the rebels executed fifteen of their prisoners, and several committed suicide rather than face capture. Garmame Neway shot his brother Mengistu to keep him from being captured, then killed himself with the same gun. Mengistu recovered but was condemned to a public hanging. Before that sentence could be carried out, in one final act of defiance, he made a speech in which he predicted that the emperor would eventually be overthrown.

Several hundred people died during the 1960 revolt, and nearly one thousand were wounded. The emperor placed thousands of rebels and students under arrest. He also dismissed several government officials he suspected of being disloyal.

Although the coup failed, many of its supporters refused to accept defeat. In the months and years that followed they continued to agitate, and gradually succeeded in permanently politicizing the people of Ethiopia.

While these internal issues kept the government in Addis Ababa preoccupied, several international and foreign policy concerns clamored for their attention as well. The most important of these was the continuing controversy over Eritrea. The Ethiopian government was interested in Eritrea for historical reasons. Prior to the nineteenth century, before it became an Italian colony, Eritrea had been part of Ethiopia. It had also been the base from which two major invasions had been launched, one in 1895–1896 and one in 1935–1936. Therefore, reunification with Eritrea would not only serve as a defensive strategy, it would also provide Ethiopia with an access to the sea. For a landlocked country having access to the sea and control over ports for shipping was better than having money in the bank.

On November 15, 1962, even though it was legally an independent country, Eritrea officially became part of Ethiopia. The new territory was called the Eritrea Province. Although this move solved several historical problems for Ethiopia, it also created a whole set of new and unexpected dilemmas. Almost immediately, many Eritreans stood in opposition to their country being unified with Ethiopia. Some of them founded their country's first militant organization, the Eritrean Liberation Front (ELF). During the coming years Ethiopian troops engaged in numerous battles with these Eritrean rebels.

The Ogaden Desert became another trouble spot for Ethiopia. In 1960 the country of Somalia, whose capital was at Mogadishu, gained its independence from Great Britain and Italy. About a million Somalis lived in Ethiopia's Ogaden Desert, beyond the border of Somalia. Many of these people

Tigre Bedouin from Rora Habab, Eritrea, c. 1900 *L. Naretti took this striking photograph in his Massawa studio, c. 1900. The Tigre people, a tribe of Muslim nomadic herdsmen, live in northwestern Eritrea. They speak Tigre, a Semitic language. A few written religious texts prepared by Christian missionary societies are the only written documents in the language.*

wanted the Ogaden to remain part of Greater Somalia. Starting in the early 1960s, there were numerous battles between Ethiopian forces and Somali rebels in the Ogaden.

Dissatisfaction with the government in Addis Ababa increased during this period. Students, especially after 1965, demonstrated against the government with increasing regularity. They focused on land reform, using the slogan "Land to the Tiller." Discontent also manifested itself in the form of several peasant revolts, primarily in the southern provinces. There was also ongoing agitation from members of Ethiopia's trade unions, who felt that their leadership was too subservient to the government.

On top of all this political turmoil, Ethiopia was struck by a terrible natural disaster. The country has always suffered from periodic famines caused by drought, but food production had been declining for several years. Between 1972 and 1974 a catastrophic famine killed several hundred thousand Ethiopians, the majority of them in the Tegray and Wallo Provinces. Not only did Haile Selassie fail to take sufficient steps to alleviate the suffering, but also the government, according to critics, tried its best to cover up the disaster.

Haile Selassie's star was beginning its slow, inexorable descent. No power on earth was great enough to halt its downward course. Its fall was as relentless as the passage of time. Haile Selassie was born July 23, 1892. He had guided his country and decided the fate of millions for six decades, from the aftermath of the "Scramble for Africa" to the age of the four superpowers, the Soviet Union, Great Britain, the United States, and France. During his reign he had watched over his country's emergence from a feudal society torn by civil war to a modern state. During the long and oftentimes treacherous journey he had witnessed two world wars, the invasion and occupation of his country, and a five-year struggle for liberation. Throughout his struggle to usher Ethiopia into the modern era, he fought hard to walk a balance beam between the old and the new, the modern and the traditional. But in recent times, the scales of progress had been tipped decidedly in his disfavor.

Almost every day there were demonstrations and complaints, and even threats. Once upon a time the people had held their emperor in high esteem. Now it wasn't safe to walk the streets. He lived virtually under house arrest. Already he had been asked by his supporters, and agreed, to hand over the responsibility of running the country to his prime minister. He watched from the Imperial Palace as talk of revolution swept through the streets of Addis Ababa, fueled by bitter resentment and opposition to his rule.

The failure of the Ethiopian government to solve the country's urgent problems was exacerbated by the drought and famine in Tegray and Wallo, which had been going on for several years when news of it broke internationally in October 1973. Reports of large-scale famine were followed almost immediately by allegations of government corruption. The famine and higher prices for food, gas, and other necessities increased the cost of living, especially in Addis Ababa. This combination of events led to an unprecedented wave of teacher, student, and taxi strikes, followed, for the first time in Ethiopian history, by mutinies in the military. They began at Negelli in Sidamo and Asmara in Eritrea and spread throughout the country.

On September 12, 1974, on the eve of the Ethiopian New Year, Emperor Haile Selassie, the two-hundred-and-fiftieth descendant of the queen of Sheba and King Solomon, was deposed. From that point forward he was officially referred to as the "ex-king" and never again as emperor. He was driven unceremoniously from the Imperial Palace in the back of a Volkswagen. As he was driven through the streets of the capital city he had helped build, Ethiopia's last emperor saw crowds of people jeering and shouting "thief" as they raised clenched fists like weapons against the falling rain. Eleven months later the eighty-three year old emperor was dead.

Ethiopian Musician, 1868   *This photograph was taken by a member of Sir Robert Napier's rescue expedition. The British Secretary of State for War donated it to the Royal Geographical Society in 1901. The man is holding a stringed* beganna. *The* azmari *of Ethiopia are noted for singing lengthy historical epics and strophic love songs to his own accompaniment on the lyrelike* beganna.

10

THE LAST EMPEROR

The future is made of the same stuff as the present.

Simone Weil (1909–1943)

After climbing a great hill, one only finds that there are many more hills to climb. I have taken a moment here to rest, to steal a view of the glorious vista that surrounds me, to look back on the distance I have come. But I can rest only for a moment, for with freedom comes responsibilities, and I dare not linger, for my long walk is not yet ended.

Nelson Mandela (b. 1918–)

With the overthrow of Emperor Haile Selassie, the three-thousand-year-old Ethiopian monarchy came to an end. A military government, the Provisional Military Administrative Council (PMAC), generally known as the *Derg,* an Amharic word for committee, replaced it. The Derg was composed of one hundred and twenty officers and enlisted men. They elected Aman Mikael Andom, a general of Eritrean descent, to serve as head of state and chairman.

The Ethiopian Revolution has been called the "bloodless revolution" because Emperor Selassie was deposed without a single shot being fired. However, it was not long before fierce and ruthless rivalries broke out among the leaders of the revolution. The first serious conflict happened when a bomb exploded in a bar frequented by Ethiopian soldiers. Some members of the Derg accused Eritrean rebels of planting the bomb and wanted to take immediate action. General Aman, on the other hand, wanted to pursue a more moderate approach. This alienated him from the more vocal members of the Derg, and they set out to teach him a lesson. On November 23, 1974, the general's house was attacked, and a gun battle followed. When it was over the general had become the first fatality of the bloodless revolution he had helped lead. A few hours later, two Derg members and fifty-seven high-ranking civilian and military officers thought to be loyal to Aman were rounded up and executed. Known as "The Death of the Sixty," this event foreshadowed a violent and uncertain future for the people of Ethiopia. It also laid to rest, once and forever, any further thoughts of Ethiopia's "bloodless" revolution.

The Derg immediately chose another officer, Brigadier-General Tafari Banti, to serve as temporary chairman and head of state. Real power, however, rested in the hands of two vice-chairmen, Major Mengistu Haile Mariam and Lieutenant Colonel Atnafu Abata. They were the men behind the scenes who made the important decisions. But over the course of the next seventeen years Mengistu would emerge as the most powerful man in Ethiopia. One by one, he eliminated those who opposed him until he held more power than an emperor. But the revolution had to advance through several stages before that happened.

In the aftermath of the changes that had taken place, many Ethiopian students and intellectuals returned to their country. They looked forward to the opportunity of rebuilding it, of correcting the terrible mistakes committed by the older generation. They were optimistic because in spite of the terrible tragedies that had taken place, there still existed an atmosphere of hope and possibility. For those who looked forward to the future, this was an exciting time.

Many of the younger generation cherished the opportunity to remake the world in their own image. They rejected the values and traditions of their fathers. In fact, many blamed the older generation for the terrible crisis that now plagued Ethiopia. As a result, they looked to new ideas and values, new heroes, and inspirations. Many of the younger generation were attracted to the ideas and philosophy of Karl Marx. For them Marxism became the answer to the problems of their country.

They grouped themselves, for the most part, into two main factions, or parties. The first was composed primarily of students and intellectuals from the north of Ethiopia, the Tegray and Wallo Provinces. Many of them had also studied in the United States. They called themselves the Ethiopian People's Revolutionary Party (EPRP). They believed in the idea of an independent Eritrea, were opposed to a military government, and advocated an immediate return to civilian rule. The second group, composed largely of Oromos, many of whom had studied in Europe, particularly France, called themselves the All Ethiopian Socialist Movement (AESM). But they were better known by the Amharic initials of MEISON. They believed that cooperation with the military, especially in the early stages, could advance the cause of socialism. Therefore, they advocated in favor of a close alliance with the Derg.

On December 20, 1974, the PMAC, with the support of MEISON, declared Ethiopia a socialist state. The following year, they carried out a series of reforms based on a concept they called *Ityopya Tikdem,* or *"Ethiopia First."* Over a hundred businesses, including banks, insurance companies, and factories were taken over by the state. Also, more than thirty thousand peasant associations were set up in an effort to deal with the poverty caused by the famine. Thousands of university and senior secondary students were sent out all over the country to organize health, literacy, and land-reform programs. These efforts did much to raise the status and self-esteem of many underprivileged members of Ethiopian society.

Yet, in spite of these achievements conflict continued among the leaders of the revolution. In February 1977 Tafari Banti, chairman of PMAC, and five other prominent members of the Derg were executed. As a result, Mengistu became Derg chairman and head of state. Soon after this meteoric rise to power, Mengistu came into conflict with MEISON, whose leaders fled the capital in July and were either jailed or killed soon afterward. Atnafu Abata, the co-vice chairman of PMAC, was later executed.

In the meantime, Somali insurgents under the leadership of the Western Somalia Liberation Front (WSLF) invaded Ethiopia. This act of aggression, and the skillful diplomacy of Mengistu, won Ethiopia the support of the Soviet Union. Up to this point the Soviet Union had been a close ally and military patron of Somalia. Now it had suddenly switched sides. In accepting help from the Russians, Ethiopia alienated the United States, which from 1953 until the overthrow of Haile Selassie had supplied Ethiopia with most of its weapons and other kinds of financial support. Thus, the unfolding of the revolution had led to a major switch in Ethiopia's international alignments.

The United States' criticism of the new regime's human rights record, coupled with Ethiopian dissatisfaction at the level of American military assistance, caused Mengistu to break with Washington, and turn increasingly toward Moscow. The social-ist states of Eastern Europe, and North Korea, were now per-ceived as valuable sources of economic and military assistance.

For Ethiopia's immediate needs this change in strategy worked well. With a steady increase of Soviet weapons, tanks, and aircraft, the Ethiopian Army went on the offensive in Feb-ruary 1978 and drove the Somalis back across the boarder. Their victory enabled them to take the offensive against the Eritrean rebels in June as well. After victories in Ogaden and Eritrea, Mengistu, by then the absolute ruler in Ethiopia, began reorganizing the country along socialist lines.

Working slowly but methodically, he established a commis-sion for organizing the Party of the Working People of Ethiopia (COPWE). The following year, the Revolutionary Ethiopian Women's Association (REWA) and the Revolutionary Ethiopian Youth Association (REYA) were set up. Then, in 1982, the All Ethiopia Peasant Association (AEPA) and the All Ethiopian Trade Association (AETA) were organized. Finally, in Septem-ber 1984, a Worker's Party of Ethiopia (WPE) was inaugurated.

These programs were designed to bring relief to the people of Ethiopia, who faced desperate circumstances due to famine and the ongoing war with Eritrea, Somalia, and political groups inside of the country. Within a three-month period of 1984, several hundred thousand Ethiopians died of hunger and disease. In 1988 Ethiopia suffered yet another famine, caused by drought and civil war. The new Socialist government tried to institute policies to ease the suffering of the millions of people caught in the terrible vice of war and famine. They introduced massive educational and literacy programs. They built hundreds of new schools, roads, health clinics, and electric facilities. The government also made efforts to help the nation's farmers, who composed nearly eighty percent of the population.

Unfortunately, because of the enormity of the problems of poverty, illiteracy, hunger, and disease, many of these policies were too little, too late. Besides, Mengistu and his followers had already sown the seeds of their own undoing in the early days of the revolution. All the deaths and political turmoil that accompanied Mengistu's rise to power had cast him in the permanent role of the evil overlord to many people in Ethiopia. So in spite of his "real" intentions, nothing was going to change the fact that he had made many enemies on his way up—the kind of enemies who were not going to rest until they saw him brought back down again.

In fact, opposition to the Derg had begun early. The murder of the prime minister and others in November 1974 was followed by several minor local rebellions. These did not attract much attention or support. However, a more broadly based rebellion came from the Ethiopian Democratic Union. Based in London, it was led by several prominent figures of the prerevolutionary past. Among these were Lieutenant General Iyasu Mangasha, an Eritrean and former Ethiopian ambassador in London. There was also Ras Mangasha Seyum, a grandson of Emperor Yohannes IV and former governor of Tegray, and Brigadier-General Negga Tagagn, a grandson-in-law of the Emperor. Their organization, which operated freely in Sudan, offered armed opposition in western Ethiopia, but was eventually defeated by the Derg.

Opposition also came from within the Socialist camp. The Ethiopian People's Revolutionary Party, which would later become the Ethiopian People's Revolutionary Democratic Front, attempted to organize urban guerrilla resistance against the Derg. In response the Derg launched a campaign known as its "Red Terror." Approximately thirty thousand Ethiopians died. As many as one thousand students in Addis Ababa were killed while passing out printed material critical of the new military government. Thousands of others were killed or put in concentration camps. This was a legacy that the new Socialist government of Ethiopia would never live down, no matter what policies it instituted to ease the suffering.

Though Mengistu's armies held their own against the liberation forces during the late 1970s and 1980s, economic difficulties, famine, drought, deaths of millions of people, not to mention the continuous, almost seemingly endless, warfare, led in due course to bitter discontent, both in the civilian and military populations. A large number of officers attempted another coup in May 1989. When it failed, Mengistu had the leaders executed. His action only intensified the discontent and opposition, especially among the soldiers who had all but laid their weapons down and refused to fight. In the meantime, the Eritrean People's Liberation Front (EPLF) and the Tegray People's Liberation Front (TPLF), took this opportunity to launch major offensives against the government of Ethiopia. Mengistu, confronted with the certain defeat and the loss of his allies in Eastern Europe, adopted a sudden change of policy. He abandoned Ethiopian socialism and took down the Soviet-built statue of Lenin. But the change was too late to have any effect. On May 21, 1991, Mengistu Haile Mariam boarded a plane first to Nairobi and then to Zimbabwe, where he was given asylum. Political instability in Zimbabwe forced him to eventually seek asylum in North Korea in 1998, where he remains to this day.

Seven days after Mengistu fled the country, the Ethiopian People's Revolutionary Democratic Front (EPRDF) took power in Addis Ababa. For the armies of liberation who had fought to overthrow Mengistu and his supporters, this was indeed a historic and triumphant moment. Their victory opened a new chapter in Ethiopia's long and varied history.

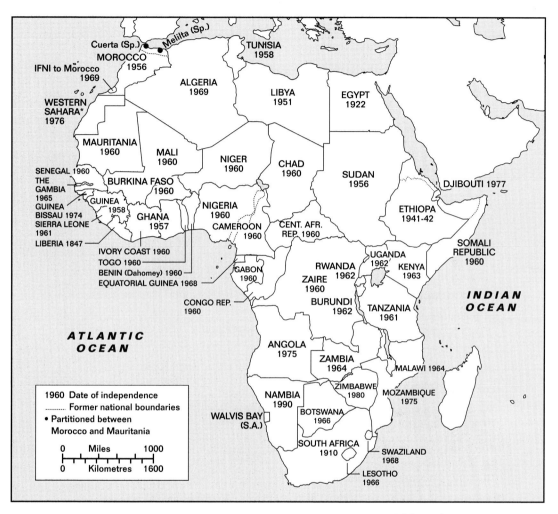

Cuerta (Sp.)
Melilta (Sp.)
MOROCCO 1956
IFNI to Morocco 1969
TUNISIA 1958
WESTERN SAHARA* 1976
ALGERIA 1969
LIBYA 1951
EGYPT 1922
MAURITANIA 1960
MALI 1960
NIGER 1960
CHAD 1960
SUDAN 1956
DJIBOUTI 1977
SENEGAL 1960
THE GAMBIA 1965
GUINEA BISSAU 1974
SIERRA LEONE 1961
LIBERIA 1847
GUINEA 1958
BURKINA FASO 1960
GHANA 1957
NIGERIA 1960
CAMEROON 1960
CENT. AFR. REP. 1960
ETHIOPA 1941-42
SOMALI REPUBLIC 1960
IVORY COAST 1960
TOGO 1960
BENIN (Dahomey) 1960
EQUATORIAL GUINEA 1968
GABON 1960
CONGO REP. 1960
ZAIRE 1960
RWANDA 1962
BURUNDI 1962
UGANDA 1962
KENYA 1963
TANZANIA 1961
INDIAN OCEAN
ATLANTIC OCEAN
ANGOLA 1975
ZAMBIA 1964
MALAWI 1964
ZIMBABWE 1980
MOZAMBIQUE 1975
NAMBIA 1990
WALVIS BAY (S.A.)
BOTSWANA 1966
SOUTH AFRICA 1910
SWAZILAND 1968
LESOTHO 1966

1960 Date of independence
.... Former national boundaries
• Partitioned between Morocco and Mauritania

0 Miles 1000
0 Kilometres 1600

Africa after Independence, 1991

The Ethiopian People's Revolutionary Democratic Front, led by Meles Zenawi, set up a national transitional government in Addis Ababa, and the Eritrean People's Liberation Front established a provisional government in Eritrea. After a referendum in 1993, Eritrea declared its independence, and Ethiopia recognized the new Eritrean government. In June 1994 Ethiopian voters elected representatives to a Constituent Assembly, charged with writing a new democratic constitution. The EPRDF won 484 out 547 seats in the assembly. A new constitution granting special rights to different ethnic groups in Ethiopia was ratified in December and became effective in August 1995. In May of the same year, a new legislature body, the Council of People's Representative, was elected with the majority of seats going to the EPRDF. In August the Constituent Assembly officially transferred power to the new legislature, and the country was renamed the Federal Democratic Republic of Ethiopia. In the same month the legislature elected Meles as the country's prime minister. He was reelected in October 2000.

In an effort to come to terms with its oftentimes painful past, the new government extended a gesture of friendship to Emperor Haile Selassie's family. On November 5, 2000, thousands of mourners lined the streets of Addis Ababa as Emperor Haile Selassie, King of Kings, Conquering Lion of Judah, and Ethiopia's Last Emperor, was finally laid to rest. He was buried in his family's crypt at Holy Trinity Cathedral, twenty-five years after his death. When he died in 1975, the emperor did not receive an official burial. In fact, it was only after the overthrow of the Mengistu regime that his remains were recovered.

For the past twenty-five years his family has tried to give Emperor Selassie a proper burial, one befitting Ethiopia's last emperor. But, for a variety of reasons they have been prevented from achieving this goal. In October, however, the new government paved the way for the funeral to take place. For the emperor's family and thousands of Ethiopians this was truly a historic moment. "I just wanted a decent burial for grandpa," said Yeshi Kassa, a great-granddaughter of the late Emperor.

Dressed in brilliantly colored robes and bearing large crosses of silver and gold, high priests of the Ethiopian Orthodox Church held a Mass outside the Holy Trinity Cathedral before solemnly leading Emperor Haile Selassie's coffin inside. The body of the emperor was then lowered into a tomb next to his beloved wife, Empress Menen. The haunting chant of Orthodox prayers echoed over the city, and thousands of people, many of them weeping, lowered their heads in prayer. Adding a few closing words to the ceremony, Yeshi Kassa stated, "This is a cathartic moment for all of us. It will certainly bring a sense of closure to the family."

At long last, the people of Ethiopia were allowed to honor their dead emperor. By paying homage to his memory, they not

Ethiopian Weaving Loom, c. 1900   *This elaborate weaving loom was photographed by L. Naretti. In some African countries, weaving is carried out by men. This man is probably one of the Doroze people of the Ethiopian Highlands, who are famed for their weaving skills. The weaving of cloth from fibers may have originated in basketmaking.*

only honored him and his family but their country's long history as well. This will certainly not be Ethiopia's final chapter. But it was a chapter that had to be written in order for the country to continue its steady march into the future. Whether or not it will prove to be another turning point for the people of Ethiopia is too soon to tell. But one thing is for certain: it was a crucial moment when the old and the new, the traditional and the modern, paused at history's crossroads to honor one of Ethiopia's greatest leaders.

WORLD WITHOUT END

DEIRDRE SHIELDS

ONE SUMMER'S DAY in 1830, a group of Englishmen met in London and decided to start a learned society to promote "that most important and entertaining branch of knowledge—Geography," and the Royal Geographical Society (RGS) was born.

The society was formed by the Raleigh Travellers' Club, an exclusive dining club, whose members met over exotic meals to swap tales of their travels. Members included Lord Broughton, who had travelled with the poet Byron, and John Barrow, who had worked in the iron foundries of Liverpool before becoming a force in the British Admiralty.

From the start, the Royal Geographical Society led the world in exploration, acting as patron and inspiration for the great expeditions to Africa, the Poles, and the Northwest Passage, that elusive sea connection between the Atlantic and Pacific. In the scramble to map the world, the society embodied the spirit of the age: that English exploration was a form of benign conquest.

The society's gold medal awards for feats of exploration read like a Who's Who of famous explorers, among them David Livingstone, for his 1855 explorations in Africa; the American explorer Robert Peary, for his 1898 discovery of the "northern termination of the Greenland ice;" Captain Robert Scott, the first Englishman to reach the South Pole, in 1912; and on and on.

Today the society's headquarters, housed in a red-brick Victorian lodge in South Kensington, still has the effect of a gentleman's club, with courteous staff, polished wood floors, and fine paintings.

AFTERWORD

The building archives the world's most important collection of private exploration papers, maps, documents, and artefacts. Among the RGS's treasures are the hats Livingstone and Henry Morton Stanley wore at their famous meeting ("Dr. Livingstone, I presume?") at Ujiji in 1871, and the chair the dying Livingstone was carried on during his final days in Zambia. The collection also includes models of expedition ships, paintings, dug-out canoes, polar equipment, and Charles Darwin's pocket sextant.

The library's 500,000 images cover the great moments of exploration. Here is Edmund Hillary's shot of Sherpa Tenzing standing on Everest. Here is Captain Lawrence Oates, who deliberately walked out of his tent in a blizzard to his death because his illness threatened to delay Captain Scott's party. Here, too is the American Museum of Natural History's 1920 expedition across the Gobi Desert in dusty convoy (the first to drive motorised vehicles across a desert).

The day I visited, curator Francis Herbert was trying to find maps for five different groups of adventurers at the same time from the largest private map collection in the world. Among the 900,000 items are maps dating to 1482 and ones showing the geology of the moon and thickness of ice in Antarctica, star atlases, and "secret" topographic maps from the former Soviet Union.

The mountaineer John Hunt pitched a type of base camp in a room at the RGS when he organised the 1953 Everest expedition that put Hillary and Tenzing on top of the world. "The society was my base, and source of my encouragement," said the late Lord Hunt, who noted that the nature of that work is different today from what it was when he was the society's president from 1976 to 1980. "When I was involved, there was still a lot of genuine territorial exploration to be done. Now, virtually every important corner—of the land surface, at any rate—has been discovered, and exploration has become more a matter of detail, filling in the big picture."

The RGS has shifted from filling in blanks on maps to providing a lead for the new kind of exploration, under the banner of geography: "I see exploration not so much as a question of 'what' and 'where' anymore, but 'why' and 'how': How does the earth work, the environment function, and how do we manage our resources sustainably?" says the society's director, Dr. Rita Gardner. "Our role today is to answer such questions at the senior level of scientific research," Gardner continues, "through our big, multidisciplinary expeditions, through the smaller expeditions we support and encourage, and by advancing the subject of geography, advising governments, and encouraging wider public understanding. Geography is the subject of the 21st century because it embraces everything—peoples, cultures, landscapes, environments—and pulls them all together."

The society occupies a unique position in world-class exploration. To be invited to speak at the RGS is still regarded as an accolade, the ultimate seal of approval of Swan, who in 1989 became the first person to walk to both the North and South Poles, and who says, "The hairs still stand on the back of my neck when I think about the first time I spoke at the RGS. It was the greatest honour."

The RGS set Swan on the path of his career as an explorer, assisting him with a 1979 expedition retracing Scott's journey to the South Pole. "I was a Mr. Nobody, trying to raise seven million dollars, and getting nowhere," says Swan. "The RGS didn't tell me I was mad—they gave me access to Scott's private papers. From those, I found fifty sponsors who had supported Scott, and persuaded them to fund me. On the basis of a photograph I found of one of his chaps sitting on a box of 'Shell Spirit,' I got Shell to sponsor the fuel for my ship."

The name "Royal Geographical Society" continues to open doors. Although the society's actual membership—some 12,600 "fellows," as they are called—is small, the organisation offers an incomparable network of people, experience, and expertise. This is seen in the work of the Expeditionary Advisory Centre. The EAC was established in 1980 to provide a focus for would-be explorers. If you want to know how to raise sponsorship, handle snakes safely, or find a mechanic for your trip across the Sahara, the EAC can help. Based in Lord Hunt's old Everest office, the EAC funds some 50 small expeditions a year and offers practical training and advice to hundreds more. Its safety tips range from the pragmatic—"In subzero temperatures, metal spectacle frames can cause frostbite (as can earrings and nose-rings)"—to the unnerving—"Remember: A decapitated snake head can still bite."

The EAC is unique, since it is the only centre in the world that helps small-team, low-budget expeditions, thus keeping the amateur—in the best sense of the word—tradition of exploration alive.

AFTERWORD

"The U.K. still sends out more small expeditions per capita than any other country," says Dr. John Hemming, director of the RGS from 1975 to 1996. During his tenure, Hemming witnessed the growth in exploration-travel. "In the 1960s we'd be dealing with 30 to 40 expeditions a year. By 1997 it was 120, but the quality hadn't gone down—it had gone up. It's a boom time for exploration, and the RGS is right at the heart of it."

While the EAC helps adventure-travellers, it concentrates its funding on scientific field research projects, mostly at the university level. Current projects range from studying the effect of the pet trade on Madagscar's chameleons, to mapping uncharted terrain in the south Ecuadorian cloud forest. Jen Hurst is a typical "graduate" of the EAC. With two fellow Oxford students, she received EAC technical training, support, and a $2,000 grant to do biological surveys in the Kyabobo Range, a new national park in Ghana.

"The RGS's criteria for funding are very strict," says Hurst. "They put you through a real grilling, once you've made your application. They're very tough on safety, and very keen on working alongside people from the host country. The first thing they wanted to be sure of was whether we would involve local students. They're the leaders of good practice in the research field."

When Hurst and her colleagues returned from Ghana in 1994, they presented a case study of their work at an EAC seminar. Their talk prompted a $15,000 award from the BP oil company for them to set up a registered charity, the Kyabobo Conservation Project, to ensure that work in the park continues, and that followup ideas for community-based conservation, social, and education projects are developed. "It's been a great experience, and crucial to the careers we hope to make in environmental work," says Hurst. "And it all started through the RGS."

The RGS is rich in prestige but it is not particularly wealthy in financial terms. Compared to the National Geographic Society in the U.S., the RGS is a pauper. However, bolstered by sponsorship from such companies as British Airways and Discovery Channel Europe, the RGS remains one of Britain's largest organisers of geographical field research overseas.

The ten major projects the society has undertaken over the last 20 or so years have spanned the world, from Pakistan and Oman to Brunei and Australia. The scope is large—hundreds of people are currently working in the field and the emphasis is multidisciplinary, with the aim to break down traditional barriers, not only among the different strands of science but also among nations. This is exploration as The Big Picture, preparing blueprints for governments around the globe to work on. For example, the 1977 Mulu (Sarawak) expedition to Borneo was credited with kick-starting the international concern for tropical rain forests.

The society's three current projects include water and soil erosion studies in Nepal, sustainable land use in Jordan, and a study of the Mascarene Plateau in the western Indian Ocean, to develop ideas on how best to conserve ocean resources in the future.

Projects adhere to a strict code of procedure. "The society works only at the invitation of host governments and in close co-operation with local people," explains Winser. "The findings are published in the host countries first, so they can get the benefit. Ours are long-term projects, looking at processes and trends, adding to the sum of existing knowledge, which is what exploration is about."

Exploration has never been more fashionable in England. More people are travelling adventurously on their own account, and the RGS's increasingly younger membership (the average age has dropped in the last 20 years from over 45 to the early 30s) is exploration-literate and able to make the fine distinctions between adventure / extreme / expedition / scientific travel.

Rebecca Stephens, who in 1993 became the first British woman to summit Everest, says she "pops along on Monday evenings to listen to the lectures." These occasions are sociable, informal affairs, where people find themselves talking to such luminaries as explorer Sir Wilfred Thesiger, who attended Haile Selassie's coronation in Ethiopia in 1930, or David Puttnam, who produced the film *Chariots of Fire* and is a vice president of the RGS. Shortly before his death, Lord Hunt was spotted in deep conversation with the singer George Michael.

Summing up the society's enduring appeal, Shane Winser says, "The Royal Geographical Society is synonymous with exploration, which is seen as something brave and exciting. In a sometimes dull, depressing world, the Royal Geographical Society offers a spirit of adventure people are always attracted to."

CHRONOLOGY

4.4 million years ago	*Australopithecus ramidus,* the world's oldest known human ancestor discovered.
3.2 million years ago	*Australopithecus afarensis,* second oldest human ancestor, better known as "Lucy" or "Demgenesh," discovered.
3546–3190 B.C.	Pharaohs of the First or Second Dynasties were in possession of myrrh, one of the most prized products obtained from Punt, possibly the eastern Tegray of modern Ethiopia.
1198–1167 B.C.	One of the last recorded pharaonic expeditions to Punt was dispatched by Ramses III.
1000 B.C.	People from Arabia cross the Red Sea into northern Ethiopia.
850 B.C.	Homer describes the Ethiopians as *eschatoi andron,* "the most distant of men."
525–456 B.C.	Aeschylus, famous Greek playwright, in his play *Prometheus Bound,* describes Ethiopia as a "land far off, a nation of black men," who lived "hard by the fountain of the sun where is the river Aethiops."
first century A.D.	Founding of Aksum Kingdom.
326	Ezana becomes King.
340	Christianity becomes official religion after Ezana is baptized.
570–632	Prophet Mohammad.
1137	Zagwe Dynasty rise to power.
1270	Yekuno Amalak, the second Solomnic Dynasty.
1530	Gragn, Muslim leader, declares Holy War.
1769–1855	Age of Princes.
1818–1868	Lij Kasa conquers Amhara, Gojjam, Tegray, and Shawa.
1855	Ly Kasa is crowned Emperor Tewodros II.
1868	Tewodros is defeated by British, commits suicide.
1872	Kasa Mucha is crowned Emperor Yohannes IV.
1889	Yohannes is killed in battle, and Sahle Mariam becomes emperor. Adopts imperial title Menelik II. Signs the Wechale Treaty.

CHRONOLOGY

1895	Italy invades Ethiopia.
1896	Battle of Adwa.
1913	Menelik II dies. Succeeded by Empress Zawditu. Ras Tafari Makonnen becomes regent.
1930	Zawditu dies. Ras Tafari Makonnen is crowned Emperor Haile Selassie I.
1935	Italy invades Ethiopia.
1941	Ethiopian Patriots, with British assistance, defeat Italian forces, liberate Ethiopia.
1952	United Nations federates Eritrea with Ethiopia.
1960	Coup to overthrow Haile Selassie.
1962	Ethiopia annexes Eritrea.
1963	First conference of the Organization of African Unity held in Addis Ababa.
1972–1974	Estimated 200,000 people die in famine.
1974	Emperor Haile Selassie dies.
1977–1979	Thousands of Ethiopians die in "Red Terror."
1977	Somalia invades Ethiopia.
1978	Ethiopia forces defeat Somalia rebels with help from Cuba and Soviet Union.
1985	Worst famine in a decade strikes Ethiopia.
1987	Mengistu elected president.
1988	Somalia signs peace treaty.
1991	Ethiopian People's Revolutionary Democratic Front captures Addis Ababa, forcing Mengistu to flee the country.
1992	Haile Selassie's remains discovered.
1993	Eritrea becomes independent.
1994	New constitution
1995	Negasso Gidadu becomes president. Meles Zenawi becomes prime minister. The country renamed Federal Democratic Republic of Ethiopia.
November 6, 2000	Haile Selassie buried in Trinity Cathedral in Addis Ababa.

FURTHER READING

Africana 2002 Encyclopedia.

Ashabranner, Brent and Mary Davis. *The Lion's Whiskers: and Other Ethiopian Tales*. Ill. Helen Siegl. North Haven: Linnet Books, 1997.

Bodker, Cecil. *The Leopard*. Trans. Gunnar Poulsen. New York: Atheneum, 1975.

Brooks, Miguel F. (trans. and ed.). *Kebra Nagast: The Glory of Kings*. Lawrenceville: The Red Sea Press, Inc., 1995.

Courlander, Harold. *A Treasury of African Folklore*. New York: Marlowe & Company, 1996.

Eiben, Therese. *"Out of Ethiopia: An Interview with Nega Mezlekia."* New York: Poets & Writers, January/February, 2002. pp. 27–33.

Encarta 2002 Encyclopedia

Encyclopedia Britannica Online.

Hancock, Graham. *The Sign and The Seal*. New York: A Touchstone Book, 1992.

Hausman, Gerald. Introduction to *The Kebra Nagast,* by Ziggy Marley. New York: St. Martin's Press, 1997.

Laird, Elizabeth. *When The World Began: Stories Collected in Ethiopia*. Oxford University Press, 2000.

Marcus, Harold G. *A History of Ethiopia*. Berkeley: University of California Press, 1994.

Millard, Candice S. *"Keeper of the Faith: The Living Legacy of Aksum."* Washington D.C.: National Geographic, July 2001. pp 110–125.

Pankhurst, Richard. *The Ethiopians: A History*. Malden: Blackwell Publications, 1998.

Scott, William R. *The Sons of Sheba's Race: African-Americans and the Italo-Ethiopian War, 1935–1941*. Bloomington: Indiana University Press, 1993.

Ullendorff, Edward. *The Ethiopians: An Introduction to Country and People*. Kingston: Headstart Printing and Publishing Company, 1998.

Ullendorff, Edward. (trans. and ed.) *The Autobiography of Emperor Haile Sellassie I King of Kings of All Ethiopia and Lord of All*

FURTHER READING

Lords. Chicago: Research Associates School Times Publications, 1999.

Van Sertima, Ivan. (ed.) *Black Women In Antiquity*. New Brunswick: Transaction Publishers, 1995.

White, Timothy. *Catch a Fire: The Life of Bob Marley.* New York: Holt, Rinehart and Winston, 1983.

There are several excellent websites for Ethiopia (http://www.imperialethiopia.org).
(http://www.addistribune.com).

INDEX

INDEX

Index

ABOUT THE AUTHORS

Dr. Richard E. Leakey is a distinguished paleo-anthropologist and conservationist. He is chairman of the Wildlife Clubs of Kenya Association and the Foundation for the Research into the Origins of Man. He presented the BBC-TV series *The Making of Mankind* (1981) and wrote the accompanying book. His other publications include *People of the Lake* (1979) and *One Life* (1984). Richard Leakey, along with his famous parents, Louis and Mary, was named by *Time* magazine as one of the greatest minds of the twentieth century.

John G. Hall received a Bachelor's degree in African American Studies and American Literature from the University of Massachusetts in Boston, and a Master's Degree in Education from Converse College in Spartanburg, South Carolina. He has contributed fiction, nonfiction, and poetry to African Voices, *Aim* magazine, *BackHome, Black Diaspora, Listen* magazine, and *The Sounds of Poetry.* John and his wife Brenda live in the mountains of Western North Carolina.

Deirdre Shields is the author of many articles dealing with contemporary life in Great Britain. Her essays have appeared in *The Times, The Daily Telegraph, Harpers & Queen,* and *The Field.*